Forces of Destiny

Christopher Bollas is one of the most expressive and eloquent exponents of the ideas, meanings and experience of psychoanalysis currently writing in English. He has a real gift for taking the reader into the fine texture of the psychoanalytic process. Here he examines and reflects on one of the most fundamental questions – what is it that is unique about us as individuals? How does it manifest itself in our personalities, our lives, relationships and in the psychoanalytic process? Drawing on classical notions of 'fate' and 'destiny' and Winnicott's idea of the true self, he develops the concept of 'the human idiom' to explore and show how we work out – both creatively and in the process of analysis – the 'dialectics of difference'. In particular he reflects on how the patients may use particular parts of the psychoanalyst's personality to express their own idiom and destiny drive.

Forces of Destiny is Bollas's second book. His first, *The Shadow of the Object* (Free Association Books, 1987), was described by the reviewer in the *International Journal of Psycho-Analysis* as a 'unique and remarkable book. I think of it as one of the most interesting and important new books on psychoanalysis which I have read in the last decade.' This book will confirm his position as one of our most important, thoughtful and engaging psychoanalytic writers.

Christopher Bollas is a member of the British Psycho-Analytical Society and the British Association of Psychotherapists. He has been Honorary Non-Medical Consultant to the London Clinic of Psycho-Analysis, Director of Education at the Austen Riggs Center, Massachusetts, and Professor of English at the University of Massachusetts. He is currently a member of the Istituto di Neuropsichiatria Infantile of the University of Rome; he is one of the literary editors of D.W.Winnicott's works and is in private practice in London.

Forces of Destiny

Psychoanalysis and Human Idiom

CHRISTOPHER BOLLAS

JASON ARONSON INC.
Northvale, New Jersey
London

First published in Great Britain in 1989 by
Free Association Books
26 Freegrove Road
London N7 9RQ

Library of Congress Cataloging-in-Publication Data

Bollas, Christopher
    Forces of destiny : psychoanalysis and human idiom / Christopher
Bollas.
      p.   cm.
    Includes bibliographical references and index.
    ISBN 0-87668-573-4 (previously ISBN 1-85343-064-1, 1-85343-065-X [pb])
    1. Self.   2. Psychoanalysis.   3. Psychotherapy—Case studies.
I. Title.
[BF697.B615   1991]
155.2—dc20   91-12363

Manufactured in the United States of America. Jason Aronson Inc. offers books and cassettes.
For information and catalog write to Jason Aronson Inc., 230 Livingston Street, Northvale,
New Jersey 07647.

For Suzanne

Greek

Idioma, a peculiarity, a specific property, a unique feature.
Idiómai, to make one's own, appropriate.
Idios, one's own, pertaining to oneself, private, personal.

(being)

Latin

Proprius, not common with others, one's own, particular.

English

Appropriate, make one's own.

(use)

Thesis

Human idiom is that peculiarity of person(ality) that finds its
own being through the particular selection and use of the object. In
this restricted sense, to be and to appropriate are one.

Contents

Acknowledgements

I am grateful to the Austen Riggs Center for the time, space, and means to write these essays.

Each of these chapters was originally a talk and I have many people to thank both for facilitating such occasions, for providing early critiques, or in some cases for reading and commenting on the final draft. Thanks to Lars Bejerholm, Ulla Bejerholm, Ken Bruder, Ed Corrigan, Bernard Ehrenberg, Darlene Ehrenberg, Andreas Giannakoulas, Adriano Gianotti, Emmanuel Ghent, Lawrence Hedges, Cecilia Jones, Marco Lombardo-Ridici, Michael Michaelocopoulos, Daniela Molina , Alexander Newman, John Padel, Laurie Ryavec, Murray Schwartz, and Marion Solomon.

My publisher, Robert Young, has provided his own unique blend of skills to keep this project moving at a good pace and I am indebted to him for his support.

Thank you to the staff of Free Association Books, to Martin Klopstock, Selina O'Grady, Wendy Millichap, and to my copy editor, Alison Wertheimer.

I owe a very special debt to my secretary, Betty Homich, who has worked tirelessly on the book.

Introduction

Psychoanalytic work is most intriguing. After years of a training analysis and the spirited if intense companionship of different supervisors, the psychoanalyst is at last delivered to his place of vocation, seated in that very particular chair, behind that even more special couch. To that place of employment the analyst brings his many acquired skills; he is equipped with cabinets of psychoanalytic models of the mind and theories of motivation and mental process, and yet, how strangely removed from obvious use these factors are when the analysand enters that space and takes up his position. It is such an amazingly complex phenomenon. Shall we ever truly understand it? I wonder.

Years ago, a patient, Jerome (described in chapter 2), taught me a great deal about the analysand's use of the elements of psychoanalysis. He did so by changing his use of me, although it is very difficult to say just in what way I changed. He got me thinking about how an analysis can provide the patient with transference objects that seem to facilitate the analysand's spontaneous expression of unthought known elements of his own character. Jerome, like many analysands, used different elements of my own personality – factors he knew to be common features of human personality – to exercise personality potentials of his own. Indeed he thrived on his uses of me by eliciting a variety of personality elements which seemed to nourish his own person establishment.

This all took place alongside ordinary essential analytic work, and I noted it, but I could never quite make sense of it. It just seemed to happen, to be important, but not analysable, as his employment of me was natural and not the action of projective identifications aimed at installing anything of himself into me. Indeed the concept of his putting into me or of my containing a part of him just didn't apply.

Time passed and my wife gave birth to our son whom I helped to look after for half of each day from his birth. What struck me was how he was who he is from scratch. He seemed to be in possession of his own personality, his own very unique configuration in being (what I term an idiom) that has never really changed in itself. He has of course taken on much more and is as complex as the rest of us due to his life with his mother and myself, but the very core of him is as it was. But what is this idiom? How does one provide evidence for it? I have been mulling this over now for some time.

Who knows how recognitions come to one. One day, while at work with an analysand, I simply realized that one of my functions for him was to be of use for his idiom moves – for private articulations of his personality potential – which could only be accomplished by eliciting different elements of my own personality. He used me well I thought. He presented a dream, indicated he wanted me just to mull it over, then suggested he wanted my associations, but not an interpretation. He also wanted an affective response and he picked a good quarrel with me. Later he drew upon my sense of humour, then my ability to recall the previous sessions and so on. I was impressed by how the uses of me seemed natural, if not conflict-free, then irrelevant to the conflict model of the self, and yet urgent. He was not primarily engaged in a form of unconscious communication, either in the narrative content or in the transference–countertransference paradigm. In fact, I think he was just living his life.

I believed I could see a link between this patient's use of me in the analysis and my son's use of his others to serve as human mediators of the articulation of the true self. It is a form of play in which the subject selects and uses objects in order to materialize elements latent to his personality, akin to a kind of personality speech, in which the lexical elements are not word signifiers but factors of personality.

This book is an effort to think about this aspect of a patient's use of the analytic situation. In part one I entertain the idea that the theory of the true self will serve as a conceptual home for some of what goes on in the clinical hour: the patient's spontaneous use of the analyst as an object. He does so, I believe, to articulate and elaborate his idiom, an accomplishment dependent on the environment's sensitive presentation of objects for such use. In psychoanalysis, the objects of use are the setting, the process, the many elements of the analyst's personality, and those ideas he contains as psychoanalytic concepts. There is an urge to articulate the true self, and I name this the destiny drive which I link up to the force of the true self to elaborate personality potential.

It is best to read part one in sequence as some of the concepts used – e.g., the destiny drive, futures, topographic return – are only spelled out clearly in their place of textual origin. The essays that form the second part of the book may be read in any order, and, although they are not an application of the theory presented in part one, each of the chapters elaborates some theoretical position taken in the first part of the book.

The reader may find the chapters in this book to be a curious mixture of established psychoanalytic theory, credible new theoretical formulations, and speculative imaginings. Further, my narrative voice moves through quite different pastures. Occasionally I outline established theory, or I work my way through to a new theoretical position, sometimes using psychoanalytic theory as the basis of consideration, at other times dwelling on clinical experiences and the psychic lives of my patients; occasionally I disclose aspects of my own history and internal life when I have no other means to convey the essence of a particular point.

Although a reader who is accustomed to a more scientific presentation of psychoanalytic work may be put off by my presentation, I hope that upon concluding the final chapter he or she will see why I express myself as I do.

I intend my writing to express something of the nature of psychoanalytic experience, which must surely be a new form of being. Perhaps we have not yet fully established a prose form to write of psychoanalytic experience, although Freud's *Interpretation of Dreams* is a model of what such prose can be. I present the reader with essays – reflective excursions of thought derived from an evolving intersection of established theory, credible new ideas, clinical encounters, self states – that constitute my way of thinking through some issue to a conclusion punctuated by this period of my knowledge, yet sufficiently inconclusive to enable me in subsequent writings to reconsider any topic presented. My imagined reader is a sympathetic one. He or she is someone who struggles to create meanings in the midst of substantial unthought knowledge, who is sometimes successful with thought, occasionally on the wrong track, but supported in this endeavour to think about clinical life by the merciful lights of futures, some knowledge of future selves and points of perspective that allow for renewed thinking and self correction.

Part One

1

A Theory for the True Self

I t is next to impossible to account for what transpires in a psychoanalysis. Although clinicians collect vignettes, remember interpretations that make sense, and isolate important psychic themes, the sheer unconsciousness of a patient–analyst relationship makes it a difficult occasion to describe. How do I talk about the qualities of silence in an hour? How can I describe the mix of tonal stress and narrative content that constitutes the analysand's unconscious emphasis of the emotional reality of a session? How shall I ever be able to narrate my inner dialogue with myself as I silently shadow the analysand, agreeing, disagreeing, querying, wondering, co-imagining? If it is possible for me to state precisely why I choose a particular interpretation, why in that moment? Why do I allow clear themes to pass without comment, only to pick up something else the patient says?

Some people find themselves incapacitated by the question 'What did you get out of your analysis?' Pressed to be specific, often by a friend who is on the verge of seeking an analyst but still needing some clear evidence of accomplishment for the considerable investment of time and money, the friend may want to know details of what was found out that was previously not known. The reply of the analysand will often be most unhelpful. 'It changed my life.' 'I was very confused and it helped to sort me out.' The unanalysed cannot be blamed for considering this a mystifying reply.

What does happen in an analysis? How can we discuss the unknown benefits of our intervention?

In some respects the history of the psychoanalytic movement can be read as a progressive effort to understand the unique situation that Freud invented and psychoanalysts inherit. Michael Balint's (1968) works on the nature of the analytic setting and the ordinary regressive features of the process, Milner's book (1969) on the role of illusion in the transference, and Winnicott's (1954) ingenious discoveries of the infant–mother memories latent to the analytic relation typify the spirit of continuing inquiry into the nature of clinical psychoanalysis within, for example, the Independent Group of the British Psycho-Analytical Society. Each of these authors believes that the success of an analysis rests not simply on the transformation of unconscious conflicts into conscious awareness, but also on fundamentally new psychic experiences generated by the analytic situation, in particular those sponsored by transference states. Naturally, some transference experiences are interpreted and cease to be unconscious, but certain uses the analysand makes of the analyst are of a different category of meaning from that represented by the concept of repressed unconscious conflict. When Winnicott introduced the term 'true self' to stand for an inherited potential that found its expression in spontaneous action, I think he conceptualized a feature of the analytical relationship (and of life) that had heretofore been untheorized.

If we explore the theory of the true self further, I think we may position ourselves to discuss previously unrepresentable features of our clinical work. I refer to that psychic movement that takes place when the analysand is free to use the psychoanalyst as an object through whom to articulate and elaborate his personality idiom. This use of an analyst is difficult to describe, but because I think it is an important part of analytical work, we must try to find a conceptual category to represent this type of psychic movement. Winnicott's theory of the true self is, in my view, just such a concept through which we may describe something we know about analysis, but have until now been unable to think.

Winnicott defined the true self as 'the inherited potential which is experiencing a continuity of being, and acquiring in its own way and at its own speed a personal psychic reality and a personal body scheme' (1960, p. 46). The spontaneous gesture was evidence of true self, and Winnicott found its earliest manifestations in the muscle erotism of the foetus. The true self was aliveness itself, and, although he saw it as an inherited potential, he did little to extend this understanding of the concept. If we are to provide a theory for the true self, I think it is important to stress how this core self is the unique presence of being that each of us is; the idiom of our personality. We are singular complexities of human being – as different in the make-up of our characters as in our physiognomies; our person design finds its expression in the discrete living villages (composed of all those objects we select to cultivate our needs, wishes, and interests) that we create during our lifetime. A genetically biased set of dispositions, the true self exists before object relating. It is only a potential, however, because it depends upon maternal care for its evolution. As its gestural expressions and intersubjective claims are never free of the other's interpretation, its evolution depends upon the mother's and father's facilitations. No human being, however, is only true self. Each inherited disposition meets up with the actual world and one of the outcomes of this dialectic between personality idiom and human culture is psychic life.

The psyche is that part of us which represents through self and object representations the dialectics of true-self negotiation with the actual world. Conflict is essential to the usefulness of the psyche which depends, in part, on the healthy balance of forces between the true self and the actual world. If a mother, for example, forecloses her infant's true self, impairing the dialectic of self and other, her infant will have a diminished psychic capability, as psychic representations owe much to the freedom of expression guaranteed by the mother and the father.

To some extent the inherited potential is objectified through self and object representations in the subject's internal world although this is always only a derivative of the true self, much as we know the unconscious through its derivatives. The idiom of the person is not, however, a hidden script tucked away in the library of the unconscious waiting for revelation through the word. It is more a set of unique person possibilities specific to this individual and subject in its articulation to the nature of lived experience in the actual world. The life of the true self is to be found in the person's experiencing of the world. The idiom that we are finds its expression through the choices and uses of objects that are available to it in the environment. If the mother knows her infant, if she senses his figural intentions, his gestures expressive of need and desire, she will provide objects (including herself) to serve as experiential elaborators of his personality potential. In this way, she assists the struggle to establish self.

The Unthought Known

That inherited set of dispositions that constitutes the true self is a form of knowledge which has obviously not been thought, even though it is 'there' already at work in the life of the neonate who brings this knowledge with him as he perceives, organizes, remembers, and uses his object world. I have termed this form of knowledge the unthought known (Bollas, 1987) to specify, amongst other things, the dispositional knowledge of the true self. More complex than an animal's instinct, which is another manifestation of an unthought knowledge, how much of this knowledge is ever to be employed and brought into the subject's being depends entirely on the nature of this child's experience of the mother and the father. If the mother and father have a good intuitive sense of their infant, so that their perception of his needs, presentation of objects for his 'use', and representation of the infant (in the face, body gestures, and language) are sensitive to his personality idiom, then he will experience the object world as facilitating. When this happens, we have children who take joy in re-presenting themselves, celebrating the arts of trans-formation because they have experienced transformative mothering and fathering and know from the authority of inner experiencing that latent knowledge can be given its life.

The Primary Repressed Unconscious

Perhaps the theory of the true self – as an inherited personality potential – is compatible with Freud's concept of the primary repressed unconscious. In 'The Unconscious', Freud wrote: 'The content of the unconscious may be compared with an aboriginal population in the mind. If inherited mental formations exist in the human being – something analogous to instinct in animals – these constitute the nucleus of the unconscious' (1915, p. 195). These 'inherited mental formations' that 'constitute the nucleus of the unconscious' – the primary repressed unconscious – may be equivalent to the idiom of the true self. Laplanche and Pontalis (1973) understand Freud's effort to conceptualize inherited schemata: 'The typical phantasies uncovered by psychoanalysis led Freud to postulate the existence of unconscious schemata transcending individual lived experience and supposedly transmitted by heredity; these he called "primal phantasies"' (p. 315).

To be sure, Freud's view of mental preformation expressed his adoption of Lamarck's theory of the genetic transmission of acquired characteristics, an argument I do not support. Human idiom is the derivative of a genetically biased disposition, but I do not know what factors suggest this determination. The experience of each foetus, inside the womb, will also contribute to the infant's personality idiom, as will birth itself. Still, if I see, as do most parents, not only physiological but personality resemblances between my child and myself, my wife, and members of our families, it is clear to me – in a most unscientific way – that my child has inherited features of his ancestral family idiom. But such a transmission need hardly be the inheritance of acquired traits, as I presume the ancestral idioms are not acquired but are derivatives of their own genetic history. This does not speak to the question of the genetic origins of idiom, but such a consideration is far beyond my capability. For me it is enough to say that infants, at birth, are in possession of a personality potential that is in part genetically sponsored and that this true self, over the course of a lifetime, seeks to express and elaborate this potential through formations in being and relating.

Freud did not develop his theory of primary repression, and used it mostly to mark the baseline in the journey of mental contents from the unconscious, through the preconscious, to consciousness. His theory of the unconscious was devoted to repression proper: to the banishment of an idea to the system unconscious. When mentioning the primary repressed unconscious, he characterized it as the domain of primary instincts that have a nucleus to them (by virtue of the repression, not as an intrinsic organization) that attracts conscious ideas, pulling them into the system unconscious and thus co-operating with the anti-cathexis exerted by the system pre-conscious to sustain repression.

If we substitute the idiom of personality (or true self) for the instincts,* as the nucleus of the primary repressed unconscious, then we can argue that the core of unconscious life is a dynamic form that seeks its being through experience. Winnicott erred, in my view, when he linked the true self to the id and the ego to the false self. He intended to emphasize the true self's representation of instinctual life, but in so doing failed to convey the organization of person that is the character of the true self. If the true self is the idiom of personality, it is therefore the origin of the ego, which is concerned with the processing of life. Naturally instincts are a part of the ego, and without delving into psychoanalytic metapsychology, I will only add that there is no reason in Freudian theory why we cannot hold that the energy of the instincts is intrinsic to and inseparable from the economics of ego life. But the drives are always organized by the ego, because this true self that bears us is a deep structure which initially processes instincts and objects according to its idiom.

If the ego is synonymous with the true self at birth, then the infant's negotiation with the mother and father establishes mental and organizational structures that subsequently become a part of the ego, but are not equivalent to the true self. The unthought dispositional knowledge of the true self inaugurates the ego, but increasingly the ego becomes an intermediary between the urges of the true self (to use objects in order to elaborate) and the counter-claims of the actual world. (This distinction is very similar to that made in classical psychoanalysis where the ego is seen as a derivative of the id, increasingly differentiated from the id as it manages the child's relation to the outside world.) We are still addressing the issue of process and not of mental representation. A part of the ego processes the demands of environmental reality, and its structure changes

---

* I do not propose that instinctual life does not exist. I simply do not give it that primacy that it holds for Freud. Somatic urges work all the time upon the mind. The drives of the id do demand expression, a task performed by the ego. But each person organizes the id differently and this unique design that each of us is is more fundamental to the choice and use of an object than the energetic requirements of the soma which themselves express the idiom of the true self.

according to the nature of the interaction with the object world. When this dialectic is thought about, the thinking occurs in the psyche, where that which is thinkable from true self experiencing is represented in the internal world.

Perhaps the primary repressed unconscious consists originally of the inherited potential and then those rules for being and relating that are negotiated between the child's true self and the idiom of maternal care. These rules become ego processes and these procedures are not thought through, even though they become part of the child's way of being and relating. They are therefore part of the unthought known and join the dispositional knowledge of the true self as essential factors of this form of knowledge. Freud's letter to Fliess of 6 December 1896 suggests that he knew there were unconscious registrations of experience not unlike theories of being and relating and he termed them conceptual memories: 'Ub [*Unbewusstsein*, unconsciousness] is the second registration, arranged according to other, perhaps causal, relations. Ub traces would perhaps correspond to conceptual memories, equally inaccessible to consciousness' (1896, p.208).

Rules stored in the primary repressed unconscious differ from the mental contents that are repressed to the system unconscious. **The secondary repressed unconscious stores thoughts** which give rise to other derived ideas as they seek disguised representation in consciousness. **The primary repressed unconscious stores processes** (of self experiencing and self–other relating) that are operationally determined in the infant's, then child's, negotiation with the mother's mothering. In *The Shadow of the Object* (Bollas, 1987) I argued that through a receptive frame of mind, a patient evokes news from within the self whereby new internal objects are created.

Perhaps this is so because the process knowledge of the unconscious ego is thought through. That is, that which has never been thought about but is a useful bit of working knowledge is mentally processed. Topographically speaking this means that through a kind of active reception to internal information the preconscious indicates interest in the unthought ideas that process both self and self–other relating. Perhaps Freud gives us a clue as to how this can happen through his theory of endopsychic perception – that mental awareness of 'the structural conditions of [our] own mind'

(Freud, 1913, p.91). Certain mental representations depict the working of the ego itself, rather like a cinema projector casting the imagery of its own internal operations on the screen. It is possible that some internalized paradigms that are part of the working structure of the ego find representation in the internal world, a projection of the workings of the ego.

In my view there are differing moments in analysis when the patient transforms process knowledge into ideation, through the representation of dream, daydream or phantasy. This may occur in a period of self-experiencing during an ordinary regression to dependence, when through a particular kind of attentiveness and due to deepening of emotional reality, the analysand transforms a scrap of unthought knowledge into its thinking. Most frequently, however, it is through the interlocking logics of the patient's transference and the psychoanalyst's countertransference, when both persons psychologically enact a process, that this knowledge is first thought about by the patient. In some respects, then, it is the paradigm potential of the transference–countertransference category that elicits unconscious rules for being and relating, and transforms these lived processes into mental representations. Indeed, the analyst's countertransference is often just such a journey of transformation from the object of the patient's process to the affective and ideational representation of the process.

In-Formative Object Relating

If unthought knowledge begins with inherited dispositions, the infant will soon know about the laws of interrelating through the relation to the mother, and this then will also become a feature of the unthought known. Such knowledge is composed of all those 'rules' for being and relating conveyed by the mother and father to the infant (then to the child) through operational paradigms rather than primarily through speech or representational thought. In other words, the child learns theories for the management of self and other through the mother's mothering. As the mother's transformational idiom alters the infant's and child's internal and external world, each transformation becomes a logical paradigm replete with complex assumptions which no infant or child can think out. These are meant to be the rules of this infant–child's existence, and they are determined by the mother's presentation of them to her infant, in interaction, of course, with his unique idiom.

As infant and mother are mutually in-formative, they act upon each other to establish operational principles derived from interrelating. Of course, the mother forms an internal object representation of her infant. But she is also in-formed by the infant's true self, so that her unconscious ego is continuously adapting to her infant. And to a far greater extent the infant is given form(s) by the mother's logic of caretaking. Object relations during the first years of life are always in-formative, so much so that such conveying of information could be termed in-formative object relating, to identify object relations that sponsor ego structures. In-formative object relating can refer either to an alteration of ego structure or to the contents of psychic life or to both. As the mother transforms the child's self states, she may induce significant ego alterations, a change in the child's processing of self and other, that may yield only minimal mental representation in the psyche. In-formative object relating at a later period of psychic development may result in the child mentally representing attitudes, actions, and other communications from the parent. This is less fateful than early in-formative object relating when the child's adaptations result in more ego change.

Signs of the True Self

A question arises. How does the analyst identify the presence of the patient's true self? Unlike the latent thoughts which constitute a manifest text, or the chain of signifiers that link the freely associated, or the familiar, if various, constellations of defences, the true self cannot be easily isolated as an object of study. A latent text, several signifiers, a network of defences can all be pointed out to a patient. As the true self is, however, only a potential, it comes into being only through experience. It does not have an established meaning (unconscious or otherwise), as its significance is contingent on the quality of object experience. Yet in the course of a clinical hour, the analyst can sense when the patient is using him to elaborate an idiom move, and, afterwards, it is possible – indeed often quite meaningful – to indicate how a patient has used one to achieve a self experience.

If the psychoanalyst has reached a decision to allow himself to be used as an object, then he is in a position to know something of the nature of such use. He knows the analysand's true self through his very particular use of those elements that constitute human personality. For example, a patient may commence a session in a lighthearted mood, initiating a relation to me based on a sense of joy. The patient may need me to facilitate this use of an element (joy) in relation to an object. Perhaps he will need, as well, my sense of humour, which I may provide (in Winnicott's sense of 'facilitate') by chuckling when the patient tells a joke or makes a wry comment on life. If the analysand's comment is amusing, then the analyst's reception to amusement is essential to the patient's use of the analyst at that moment. This is indicative of true self use of the analyst, where the patient is using the analyst's sense of irony, or sense of humour. If the patient's comments constituted an effort to be ironic and amusing, then more likely than not, the communication is evidence of false self and the analyst's sense of irony or humour will not be inspired and therefore not used. Perhaps the analyst's senses of awkwardness or irritation will be evoked by such a false self act and this may complement the patient's own discomfort.

Perhaps a patient becomes highly articulate, evoking the analyst's capacity to interpret unconscious communications. The analyst, then, is used for his ability to concentrate and bring his analytic intellect to bear on the task. This could constitute a movement of true self as it uses the object.

On another occasion a patient, perhaps after reporting a dream and its associations, searches for the analyst's sense of intellectually creative freedom. He inspires the analyst's free associations. Such associative freedom might be warranted one moment in working on a dream and then not be correct on another occasion when the patient wants the analyst to 'hold' the dream and its associations, needing the analyst to be in a quiet and reflective state.

The aim of these reflections is to suggest an important clinical differentiation in the patient's use of the analyst. **True self use of an analyst is the force of idiom finding itself through experiences of the object.** Although at times such idiomatic use of the analyst may reveal patterns of personality, the analysand's aim is not to communicate a

re David attempts to be T for S - Analyze - when
he begins to feel too strongly... need to forgive
or absense of forgiveness = no appreciation. Forgiveness
for what? - What father did? What a David's father?

A Theory for the True Self

child–parent paradigm script, but to find experiences to establish true self in life. At other times, however, a patient does indeed create an object relation to convey some rule for being and relating derived from his relation to the mother or father.

As I have argued that the ego is the unconscious organizing process – the logic of operations – its choices will ultimately reflect both the innate true self (an organization that is its precursor) and the subsequent structures developed out of partnership with the mother and father. Therefore any ego operation in adult life will inevitably be some kind of mix of true self and true self's negotiation with the world. There is no pure culture of true self, just as there is no unmediated presence of the mother's structure of caretaking. Clinically, however, we see uses of the analyst substantially more on the side of true self movement which will override our immediate consideration of any related ego structure. The meeting point of the two factors in an analysis (of true self and internalized object relations) is often when true self movement is arrested by some paradigmatic diversion (or distortion) that is represented in the transference.

How does the analyst know how to distinguish a true self use of him from a paradigmatic use? The clue, I think, rests in the internal information provided in the countertransference. When an analyst is used to express a paradigm derived from an object relation, he is coerced into an object relation script and given a certain sustained identity as an object. He is 'set up' to play a part in the completion of a role that has become an ego operational paradigm. When, however, this does not occur, when an element is elicited in him to be used by the patient and then abandoned (with no aim to set the object up as part of the logic), then, in my view, this is more likely to be a true self movement to its experience through the object.

Are these systems of knowledge always distinguishable? I think not. As the mother operationalizes the infant's true self into the infant–mother object relationship, true self becomes part of the dialectic of interrelating. A true self idiom move will become part of a relationship. But in the first months of life, a good enough mother facilitates the infant's true self, so he experiences object-seeking as useful. If, on balance, a patient's use of the analyst is useful, where transference experience is sought in order to elaborate the core of the ie Repeated 'put down' of S. for not forgiving ? for staying to her pain + separateness & not David. David shifts to Natalie (wants to) became to stay in his pain would kill him (not Natalie's death)

self, then the clinician will not attend to the self–object paradigms latent in any segment of such use. Only when a pattern establishes itself, when a complex of uses is repeated, does the analyst shift attention to consider the laws implied in this category of unthought knowledge.

It is possible then to say that much of what occurs in an analysis has not been articulated or thought before. Indeed, it is perfectly natural that this should be so as until the invention of psychoanalysis (so far as I am aware), there was no cultural space for the articulation of the unthought known in quite this careful manner. While I think it is possible for the psychoanalyst to understand and interpret those theories of being and relating that typify an analysand's approach to life, it is difficult, in my view, to see the journey taken by the true self in the analysis. Of course, there are many times when we sense that we are being used to process an idiom move, we know that some of our interpretations have a particular transitional function for the patient but such lucidity, significant though it is, is a derivative of that deep, silent, profoundly unconscious movement taken by the true self and effected, with equal unconsciousness, upon ourselves. We can analyse the rules for being and relating when they are recreated in the transference and its countertransference, but we cannot analyse the evolution of the true self. We can facilitate it. We can experience its momentary use of our self. We can identify certain features. But we cannot 'see' it all of a piece, in the way that we 'see' what unconscious meaning there is that lies hidden in the narrative text. To some extent this is because it exists only in experience and is contingent upon the nature of experience to trigger idiom moves. Perhaps we need a new point of view in clinical psychoanalysis, close to a form of person anthropology. We would pay acute attention to all the objects selected by a patient and note the use made of each object. The literature, films, and music a person selects would be as valued a part of the fieldwork as the dream. Photos of the interior of the analysand's home, albums chronicling the history of domestic object choice, dense descriptions of their lovers, friends, enemies might assist us in our effort to track the footsteps of the true self. But I fear we should know only a bit more than we otherwise would were no such effort made, as the choice of objects tells us little about the private use of the object. As I shall

18

How relates to sand work – ? How Pt. makes 'private' use of obj.. may have nothing to do in "tray" as whole. ie. David uses objects (here) to build struct. y persons 'room' (house). (flowers, cars to latest!)

explore in chapter 5, it is possible for an analyst to note how he has (or has not) been used by a patient, and to comment on how a patient's very particular use of the analyst, at a moment in the session, expressed a feature of this analysand's true self.

Although Winnicott's theory of an inherited disposition is related to Melanie Klein's theory of instinct (1952) as possessing an innate knowledge of the relation to the object (as for example the relation to the breast), his use of the concept to identify the inner originating source of the spontaneous gesture and my view that the true self exists through the use of an object suggest a different emphasis. The concept of idiom, to specify the unique personality potential of each individual – a potential that is only partly articulated through the experiencing of a lifetime – emphasizes the innate factor as a personality theory rather than simply as a universal phylogenetic knowledge. I agree that such phylogenetic knowledge of the breast, perhaps of the face, perhaps of the father, does exist, but it is more accurate to say that such phylogenetic knowledge is only a part of the inherited factor, as I think infants inherit elements of their parents' personalities by virtue of the genetic transmission of genetic structure.

To some extent, Bion's theory of 'preconception' (1962) emphasizes that need for experience defined by Winnicott as essential to realization of the true self. Infants are born with innate preconceptions, according to Bion, which, through experience that matches a preconception, lead to realizations that foster a conception. The true self is a highly complex idiom of personality preconceptions that come into realization through experiences in life that resonate with the preconception. As such, certain experiences in life feel incredibly valid or important to the person as they seem to register the essence of the self.

In fact, when an experience arrives to express the true self, the individual is able to be spontaneous, to be tru(er) in that moment. The ordinary joy, found by linking a true self preconception with the object world, is a very special form of pleasure. I think of this factor as well served by the word *jouissance*, which is an important part of Lacan's (1960) formulation of psychoanalysis. *Jouissance* is the subject's inalienable right to ecstasy, a virtually legal imperative to pursue desire. Perhaps this is a good definition of the ruthless pleasure of the human subject to find joy in the choice and use of the object. Indeed, there is an urge to use objects through which to articulate – and hence be – the true self, and I term this the destiny drive, a topic which I discuss in the next chapter.

Essential Aloneness

Something of what Winnicott (1963) means by the isolate that we are is determined by this true self. Shadowing all object relating is a fundamental and primary aloneness which is inevitable and unmoveable. And this aloneness is the background of our being; solitude is the container of self.

In his book *Human Nature* (1988) Winnicott poses the following question: 'What is the state of the human individual as the being emerges out of not being? What is the basis of human nature in terms of individual development? What is the fundamental state to which every individual, however old and with whatever experiences, can return in order to start again?' (p. 131). He replies: 'A statement of this condition must involve a paradox. At the start is an essential aloneness. At the same time this aloneness can only take place under maximum conditions of dependence' (p. 132).

Essential aloneness is a positive term for Winnicott, an isolation that is supported by a human environment. As this aloneness characterizes the environment out of which being emerges, we carry it with us through life. Before aloneness, according to Winnicott, is 'unaliveness': 'the experience of the first awakening gives the human individual the idea that there is a peaceful state of unaliveness that can be peacefully reached by an extreme of regression' (p. 132). This aloneness is a transitional state between unaliveness and aliveness characterized by dependence and instinctual life. For Winnicott, 'the recognition of this inherent human experience of pre-dependent aloneness is of immense significance' (p. 133).

Perhaps one day we will discover that we possess existence memories, that our experiences become a part of our being which itself is a form of remembering, and which in turn is available for transformation into representation through imagination, such as in the dream. If so, foetal experiences become part of our being, and are available for mental elaboration through the imagery of dreams and phantasies which represent it.

In the long evolution of the foetus, from its pre-organic history (in the genetic make-up of the parents) to its birth, and then in the dramatically progressive evolution of the infant in those first two years, prior to speech, the human being lives a profoundly dependent life, at first literally inside the mother, then inside the postnatal interrelation – and all of this lived before speech. The progression from prenatal essential aloneness to the adult's capacity to be alone (the action of Winnicott's 'isolate') testifies to our early self, to the experience of the idiom of the true self, finding its trueness through movement pleasures (prenatal and postnatal) that exist in a precultural category of significance; its subsequent elaborations, though certainly using cultural objects, serve its own pleasure in articulating itself, rather than in understanding and conveying the meaning of the cultural objects used. The true self listens to a Beethoven sonata, goes for a walk, reads the sports section of a newspaper, plays basketball, and daydreams about a holiday – not to know these 'objects' and then to cultivate this knowledge into a communication, but to use these objects to yield self experiences. (Of course the use of an object will yield information about it. What we learn from object use becomes immediately available to another category of human experience: the repressed unconscious.)

In our true self we are essentially alone. Though we negotiate our ego with the other and though we people our internal world with selves and others, and though we are spoken to and for by the Other that is speech (Lacan's theory of the Symbolic) the absolute core of one's being is a wordless, imageless solitude. We cannot reach this true self through insight or introspection. Only by living from this authorizing idiom do we know something of that person sample that we are.

In some respects psychoanalysis is a place for the experiencing of essential aloneness. There is a *Waiting for Godot* silence to many analytic hours. The experienced analysand, dispensing with that pre-sessional foreknowledge typical of the novice patient (who is anxious to prove worthy of the analyst's concentration), lingers on the couch, just waiting. Inside the darkened and mute theatre of the mind

21

he remembers having had a dream the night before. But he does not recall the dream. Instead he 'sees' the darkness, recalls the psyche–soma at night, and rests now in the shadows of that non-existence that we are between the acts of the dream. Or he has a brief sense of a forgotten memory. He does not recollect the memory, he senses its unremembered presence. He waits for it to show up, if it will. This waiting-about mirrors that interval inside the self, as we rest between psychic registrations, like cinema-goers who see a film clip, then face a darkened and empty screen. The darkened screen is as much a part of our life as is the play of images across its illumined surface. We are as often waiting in the interiors of silence and darkness as we are informed by the projections of psychic news. There, in that solitary space, we repeatedly contact that essential aloneness that launches our idiom into its ephemeral being.

beautiful

2

The Destiny Drive

The psychoanalytic process contains within it two seemingly opposed elements: a deconstructive procedure and an elaborative process. The patient brings a dream, a scrap of narrative, a random thought, and the analyst, by asking for associations, breaks down the manifest text of the material to reveal the unconscious latent content. In some respects this is an act of destruction, and most analysts are well accustomed to the patient's initial distress over having his manifest context (his word) deconstructed in this manner. In time, however, the patient not only accustoms himself to this dismantling of his discourse, but soon joins in the process. Analyst and patient then engage in a mutual destruction of manifest texts to voice the latent thoughts of the repressed unconscious.

Interestingly, such deconstruction is possible only if the analysand elaborates latent thoughts through the semantic migrations of free association. Perhaps such elaborations are themselves deconstructions as the ceaseless waves of displaced signifiers, seeming to represent a vast sea of meanings, leave traces in the sand, to reveal the secrets of this other world. If so, analysis needs the fecund elaborations provided by free association, a movement away from the latent unconscious, in order to suggest the secret sub-text. To dismantle the patient must construct. To find the truth all patients must lie.

Another elaborative feature of the analytic process is the patient's transference.

Psychoanalysis as an Elaboration of True Self

The patient's unconscious use of the psychoanalyst in the transference is seemingly an elaborative rather than a deconstructive process, as the analysand cumulatively constructs his object world through the person of the analyst. If the dismantling of the dream's manifest text illuminates the analytical side of the psychoanalytic process, the articulating of the transference exemplifies the elaborative factor. A patient begins analysis with some transference idea of the analyst, perhaps an avuncular figure. In the months to follow he experiences the analyst differently according to the varying elements of his personality. Of course, the transference uses of the analyst, like the free association to the dream text, are a deconstruction, a dismantling of the analyst's 'true' or 'manifest' personality. And the establishments of transference have a constructive logic. Just as dream analysis unveils a chain of signification through free association, so too the analysand reveals through the transference the psycho-logical affiliations between elements of the mother's, father's, and child selves' personalities, engaged as they were in living and creating a life together. As a personality field, the analyst is also used to elaborate the analysand's idiom, but this is less easily objectified than the patient's dream report or transference construction.

In some respects, however, the analyst's mental relation to these two factors – the deconstructive and the elaborative – is different. In breaking down manifest texts, he searches the material to discover important signifiers of meaning. As a transference figure, he is used as an object, and his mental state is receptive rather than analytic. Winnicott wrote of a 'natural evolution of the transference' and suggested that this process should not be disrupted by the 'making of interpretations'. He did not mean that the analyst should not interpret: he meant that the analyst should not be engaged in making interpretations. By stressing the making of interpretation as disruptive, he acknowledged that sometimes we feel obliged to make an interpretation because we imagine this to be our task as analysts. And the 'making' of an interpretation may preoccupy the analyst for the better part of a session, interfering with his more receptive frame of mind.

Clearly, if the transference is viewed as partly a natural and evolving process, then psychoanalysis sets in motion a constructive articulation of the patient's object world. The analyst's task here, at least as Winnicott viewed it, is to give the patient time to establish and articulate his internal world. This, of course, does not necessitate abandonment of the deconstructive procedure in analysis. In fact, mental life is sufficiently complex and sophisticated to embrace such a relatively small contradiction. We can continue to ask for the analysand's associations and break down his manifest texts without disturbing the evolution of the transference which moves in a different category of signification.

But in dwelling on these two different valences of the analytical procedure – deconstruction and elaboration – I think we can say that the deconstruction of the material as an object is part of the search for meaning, and the elaboration of the self through the transference is part of the establishment of meaning. The need to know and the force to become are not exclusive, but the latter element of the analytic process has received less attention that it deserves and is my focus now.

The True Self and the Use of the Object

By allowing the patient to use him as an object in the transference, Winnicott facilitated the establishment of self states, many of which had only been a possibility. He understood the analytic situation to be a potential space. Its potential was largely the analyst's creation. If the analyst was inattentive to the patient's need to create his own transference object, then analytic practice, of sorts, existed, but one could not speak of potential space. Through the illusions of the transference, the patient could bring into life elements of the mother, the father, siblings, and parts of his child self. Bringing to life is an important feature of the nature of the transference. There is a difference between talking about the mother, the father, and former child selves, and *being* the mother or father or a child self. Only by being someone or something is the patient able to establish elements of the self in psychoanalysis.

In his complex and interesting paper 'The use of an object', Winnicott (1969) wrote that the infant's capacity to use an object followed on his ability to relate to the object. To some this seems a callous reversal of priorities. How can using someone be maturationally more promising than relating to someone? It's a fair question, but relating to the object refers to the depressive position, and the infant's anxiety about harming the object. In the depressive position, the infant realizes his hate could harm the (internal) love object, and reparative work is necessary to repair the internal object although, of course, this also involves actions in the actual world.

The concept of the use of the object assumes that the child has a fairly secure sense of his love of the object so that hate is allowed without decomposing the ego or its objects. This internal work allows for appreciative recognition that the actual object has, in any event, survived its own destruction as an internal object. The survival of the actual object is both a relief and a new beginning. The child knows now that he can assume his love of the object in order to use it (in phantasy and in reality) without concern about its well-being. 'Because of the survival of the object,' Winnicott writes, 'the subject may now have started to live a life in the world of objects, and so the subject stands to gain immeasurably' (p. 90).

What does it mean to 'live a life in the world of objects'? Do we not all live in a world of objects? Do we know of anyone who does not? The issue Winnicott addresses can only be understood if we grasp that he does not assume that we all 'live' a life. We may construct the semblance of such and certainly the false self attests to this. But to live a life, to come alive, a person must be able to use objects in a way that assumes such objects survive hate and do not require undue reparative work.

Relationship as a defence against usage can be seen most clearly in the life of sexual couples. In lovemaking, foreplay begins as a act of relating. Lovers attend to mutual erotic interests. As the economic factor increases, this element of lovemaking will recede somewhat (though not disappear) as the lovers surrender to that ruthlessness inherent in erotic excitement. This ruthlessness has something to do with a joint loss of consciousness, a thoughtlessness which is incremental to erotic intensity. It is a necessary ruthlessness as both lovers destroy the relationship in order to plunge into reciprocal orgasmic use. Indeed the destruction of relationship is itself pleasurable and the conversion of relating to using transforms ego libido into increased erotic drive. If a couple cannot assume this essential destructiveness, erotic intensity may not give in to mutual orgasm. Instead, reparation may be the fundamental exchange between such couples with partners entering into prolonged mother–child scenarios, of cuddling, holding, or soothing. This may be because such persons have not been able to experience a good destruction of the object, and reparative work is activated during the arrival of instinctual urges. When this happens, sexual uses of the object may be enacted as dissociated activities. Instead lovers may masturbate each other, with one partner relating to the other's sexual needs and mothering them through it, or at an extreme, in the perverse act, the couple may wear interesting garments and introduce curious acts to entirely split off the destructive side of erotic life, in a kind of performance art.

In some ways the analytic relationship is akin to the above relation of lovers. Some analysands are so frightened by their destructive phantasies, or, by the effect of such feelings, by a fear of being torn to pieces by the analyst, that they cannot bring themselves to use the analyst as an object. This may show up ironically enough in the form of a continuous self-analysis, with the patient rigorously analysing himself in the presence of the analyst whom he seeks, if anything, as a supervisor. Or the patient may simply, as we know, keep silent about the more disturbing feelings and talk about something removed from the person of the analyst.

But there are patients who seem to have an uncanny ability to use us as an object in the transference. By discussing one patient briefly I think I can make this point clear.

Jerome

Jerome was a stocky East European man in his mid-forties when he came for analysis. He had been in psychotherapy for some years and had previously sought analysis, but had been refused because he was considered too paranoid for analytic treatment. When I saw him, it was true that he was harassed by ideas of reference, and many sessions were filled with preoccupations about what other people were thinking about him, or saying about him, and how he was going to gain his revenge. Analytic hours became painstaking reports on

27

how someone had slighted him and what he had done to retaliate, or what he would do to continue his campaign against the person. Whenever possible, I would make an interpretation in the transference, but he insisted that he trusted me and that he was not suspicious of me. Over time he became more critical of me, saying that I lived with certain analytical prejudices which he found unfortunate. One such prejudice was to have in my mind the idea that he suffered a depression; he did not want me to talk about his hate leaving him depleted, because he experienced the interpretation itself as contaminating him with the very affect I described. This led to a useful period of working on how he needed to preserve me as an unreal object in order to protect himself against an imagined revenge on my part.

But the fact was that his narratives were conveyed from the same self state, day in and day out. He was always tentative, anxious, intense, and somewhat irritable. He reported events in the same manner, listened to what I said carefully, usually did not reply, or agreed, and then would proceed to talk about something else. While I could persuade myself that I was analysing the patient's transference to me, that I was putting it into words, including sharing my sense that he was keeping a certain psychic distance from me, the fact is that I became troubled by the rut we seemed to be in.

Then one day Jerome changed the course of his analysis. He came to a session with a smile on his face and chuckled to himself as he lay on the couch. I commented on this, and he seemed anxious and uncertain about what to say. I noted this and said that whatever it was he had thought, it seemed to have left him worried. He then spent some time trying to talk but not talk about what had been on his mind. He told me that he had been thinking about the patient who had preceded him. As he did so, he suggested that he had mixed feelings about the patient and told me about his previous therapist who had interpreted to him often about his sibling rivalry. As he talked about this, the image of the previous patient came to my mind, and the idea of rivalry did too. But these discourses still did not feel right to me. I concentrated on his chuckle and said that nonetheless he seemed to have gained some amusement from the previous patient: did he intend to keep this pleasure to himself? I said this in a playful manner. I am sure that I worded it this way because he was ready for a comment such as this, and then Jerome told me the truth. On the way to his hour, while passing by the door by which patients leave, he had had an impish thought. He wondered what I would do if he knocked on the door. He imagined that I would open the door to find him wearing cowboy boots and a Stetson hat. He would then rather awkwardly peer into the room, introduce himself to the patient (whom he imagined to be a woman) and say in a Texan drawl, 'Well, how de do Dr Bollas! Be seeing you for one of our great meetings just as soon as you're finished with the little lady here.'

And that was it. I found his daydream aptly funny and I laughed. Even in reporting the fantasy, the patient had been quite worried by my response, but he was greatly relieved that I had found it funny. I told him why I found it amusing. Here he imagined something that clever I certainly could not interpret my way through. Yes, it would certainly be an impossible moment for me! I congratulated him on his invention. He then embellished the idea of surprising me and for the next two weeks he would come to sessions with yet another story of putting me in a difficult situation, one that inevitably caused him great humour. And I must say, I found these vignettes funny.

The point is that he quite changed within himself through his imaginary use of me. He was still somewhat hesitant, but he was more confident than I had seen him before, and much more likeable. His paranoid thoughts and revenge plots diminished over the next few months until they completely disappeared. He found his way to create an imaginary me, and then through more direct expressions of feeling, disagreement, anger, and difference, he established different self states in my presence. I do not mean to suggest that these were either unconscious or conscious roles that he enacted. He had rarely forcefully disagreed with anyone. This had left him in a very frustrated and highly mentated world with aggression becoming omnipotent destructiveness. So when he 'abused' me in phantasy by making me ridiculous, which I enjoyed, he discovered a pleasure in aggression. Eventually, he would disagree forcefully with interpretations that I made and he did so with a clarity and acuity of perception that had been missing.

If we view this from a certain perspective, then it's possible to say that through my willingness to be used as an object, announced in some respects through a very slight though different playfulness in my orientation to his presence, the patient was able to invent me anew in the sessions. As I desisted from interpreting the content of his imagining and instead simply took pleasure in his inventions, I believe I created a certain freedom for him to play without such activity being prematurely moved into the domain of analytical reflection. This seemed to announce to the patient that it was now quite safe for him to change his use of me as an object. Perhaps the months of interpretive work had gained effect. The patient could now play with the analyst, his prior persecutory anxieties having been worked through. The fact that I responded to the slightly different use of me facilitated his spontaneous articulations. He could forget how I felt, he could abandon his worry about whether he was damaging me, and he could forget being serious as a way of forestalling any imagined revenge on my part. He was able to do this because in effect, as the object, I announced, 'I'm capable of a change of use'.

My willingness to be imagined evoked a different unconscious aim in the patient. Whereas before we can say that the aim was to understand his internal object world and to learn something of his mental processes, the new aim in the sessions was to set aside that priority in order to act. Such acting was a means of establishing domains for true self articulations.

For example, many months later, when we had time to reflect on his many imaginings, we could see that the Texan with the Stetson reflected a choice of object determined by his personal idiom. As a boy he played at being a cowboy who strode about the streets of his neighbourhood. I think it signified confidence and phallic capability. In the context of the session, viewed from a transference perspective, it indicated oedipal rivalry with me.

The patient had to be ruthless in his use of me. He had to be beyond concern. In this I think he was assisted by my slight celebration of his right to destroy me. I think that this ability to enjoy destroying me was partly accomplished through interpretive work that had accomplished an internal structural change in the patient. But he was further enabled to destroy me without inner persecution because I enjoyed it. What I did is not dissimilar from what a good enough mother does when she celebrates the infant's aggression. And, of course, my celebration of him was a symbolic act, rather than a literal act of mothering, the paradigm of aggression as acceptable was communicated to him unconsciously, and as soon as he understood this, he changed. It actually occurred within one session.

To be sure, this therapeutic experience would in and of itself be insufficient to effect a lasting psychological change. When the patient was ready for it, we looked back on what had happened and analysed my contribution to the change, his response to it, his use of me, and how this enabled him to be aggressive without persecution. But with this good enough experience inside him, I think the patient had that kind of self that could then work more fruitfully with ordinary analytic interpretation. He did not feel deprived by insight but enhanced by it. Before, even though he rarely alluded to it, he often felt that I somehow diminished him by interpreting his destructiveness, and he felt despair about his future.

On the Differentiation of Fate and Destiny

In considering the elaborative factor of a psychoanalysis, I find it useful to consider the idea of destiny and to distinguish a person's sense of destiny from his sense of fate. In classical literature, fate and destiny tend to be used synonymously, although occasionally we can observe some difference in their use. In the *Aeneid*, Juno calls upon the fates to intervene on her behalf against Aeneas, but her wishes are thwarted because Aeneas' destiny does not permit such an intervention. This brings to mind an interesting distinction between the two concepts. I have not found a single instance in classical literature where destiny intervenes as a capricious or destructive act on the part of one of the gods. The course of destiny can be altered, but this is usually through the epic hero's interpretation of his destiny. On the other hand fate, or the fates, do intervene quite often, and it's possible to speak of capricious fates. Not until the seventeenth century do we observe an increasing differentiation between these terms, when destiny becomes a more positive concept depicting that course that is a potential in one's life. One can fulfil one's destiny if one is fortunate, if one is determined, if one is aggressive enough. Possibly the idea of fate derives from an agrarian culture where people are dependent on the seasons and the weather for their nurturance, thus giving man a sense that his life is very much up to the elements. If this is true, then destiny as a positive factor may be linked with the rise of the middle class as individuals who, through vision and labour, are able to take some control of their lives and chart their future.

Fate derives from the Latin *fatum* which is the past participle of *fari* which means to speak. 'Fatum' is 'a prophetic declaration', and 'fatus' is an oracle. Webster's *New Twentieth Century Dictionary* states that fate is 'The power supposed to determine the outcome of events before they occur'. This is an interesting definition and helps us to differentiate between the meaning of fate and of destiny. If we review the classical literature, I think that we will find that fate is usually announced through an oracle, or the words of a person, as, for example, when Oedipus' fate is spoken by the oracle of Apollo at Delphi. Oedipus' destiny, however, is determined by the chain of events that the oracle announces. Destiny, from the Latin *destinare*, means to fasten down, secure, or make firm, and the word destination is a derivative of this root. Thus destiny is linked to action rather than words. If fate emerges from the word of the gods, then destiny is a pre-ordained path that man can fulfil. I think it is of interest that one of the clearest distinctions between these terms emerges in the twentieth century in *The American College Dictionary* which states:

> *Fate* stresses the irrationality and impersonal character of events: 'it was Napoleon's fate to be exiled'. The word is often lightly used, however: 'it was my fate to meet him that very afternoon'. *Destiny* emphasizes the idea of an unalterable course of events, and is often used of a propitious fortune: 'a man of destiny'; 'it was his destiny to save his nation'.

What place do these terms have in a psychoanalysis? The person who is ill and comes to analysis either because of neurotic symptoms, or characterological fissures, or psychotic ideas and pains, can be described as a fated person. That is, he is suffering from something which he can specify and which has a certain power in his life to seriously interfere with his capacity to work, find pleasure, or form intimate relationships. And we could say that the classical symptom is a kind of oracle: figure it out, unravel it through associations and the discovery of its latent meaning, and one can be free of that curse which its unknownness has sponsored. But along with the fate a person brings to analysis is a destiny which can only be a potential whose actualization depends less on the sleuth-like unravelling of the oracular symptomatology or the dream, than it does on the movement into the future through the usage of the object, a development that psychoanalysts term the transference.

In endeavouring to use these two concepts in a psychoanalytic sense, I must create further distinctions between them. I believe we can use the idea of fate to describe the sense a person may have, determined by a life history, that his true self has not been met and facilitated into lived experience. A person who feels fated is already someone who has not experienced reality as conducive to the fulfilment of his inner idiom. Thus I can link the sense of fate to the concept of the false self and to Winnicott's idea of reactive living. And such a person, frustrated at the very core of his being and relating, will project into his internal objects split-off aspects of this true self, thus giving to internal objects a certain further power to fate his life. Indeed, classical man's fate, mediated through an oracular voice, may be based on split-off parts of the self preserved as hallucinations. The intervention of fate would, then, be a return of a split-off part of the self (or other).

It is to the idea of destiny that I now turn. We can use this concept to address the evolution of the true self, to ask of any individual whether or not he is fulfilling his destiny. There is, as I have said, an urge to establish one's self. This destiny drive is that force imminent to the subject's idiom in its drive to achieve its potential for person elaboration. Through mental and actual objects this idiom seeks to articulate itself through the 'enchainments' of experience.

Idiom and Destiny

For classical man, a sense of destiny would refer to the parts of the self that have not been split off and remain 'inside' the subject, giving him a sense of being on the right track. To some extent, then, heredity, biology, and environment are factors contributing to one's destiny. A mother can either be fundamentally a fateful presence or an object through whom the infant establishes and articulates aspects of his destiny. What do I mean by this?

By sustaining the infant's illusion that he creates his world, the mother, from Winnicott's point of view, enables the infant to experience his objects as subjective in origin. Thus object orientation and subsequent object relating emerge from this primary experience that objects derive from one's creativity. Naturally the infant will actually be disillusioned, both by the mother's ordinary failures and by the many lessons culled from reality, but the illusion of primary subjectivity will not completely disappear. In my view, it simply means that the infant, the child, and then the adult will carry an internal sense of creating his own life, even if the structures of society, the laws of one's culture, and the course of events cannot possibly be said to evolve out of the subject's true self. But the maternal provision of an illusion of creativity, which sponsors an experience but not a sense of omnipotence, marries up with the destiny drive which we can think of as an internal sense of personal evolution through space and time. After all, in some ways, this is what developmental theory is about: an evolution that traces the progressive maturation of the individual.

A sense of destiny, then, would be a feeling that the person is fulfilling some of the terms of his inner idiom through familial, social, cultural, and intellectual objects. I believe that this sense of destiny is the natural course of the true self through the many types of object relations and that the destiny drive emerges, if it does, out of the infant's experience of the mother's facilitation of true self movement. The true self, as Winnicott suggested, can evolve through maternal adaptation and responds to the quality of care the child receives from the mother and the father, as well as from the school and the peer world. Does the object world, in other words, provide the right conditions for the child to evolve his idiom, to establish his personality in such a way as to feel both personally real and alive, and to articulate the many elements of his true self?

Destiny

When Freud wrote of endopsychic perception – an ability to visualize the inner workings of the subject's mind – he argued that such perceptions were projected into objects to form, for example, the structure of myths. In *Totem and Taboo* (1913) he said that myths partly described the structure of the human mind.

We may certainly wonder if those factors in the ego that make endopsychic perception and projection possible also work on the true self, to, as it were, perceive the potential idiom that we are, and to project it in dreams, personal myths, daydreams, and visions of the future. Endopsychic projection of our idiom means that we are ever so slightly led by our projections, that we have a sense of direction built into our existence. (This loss of a sense of direction might help us to understand psychotic patients who often project the loss of an inner sense of direction.) Perhaps if the child is living from the true self, if his right to *jouissance* is sustained by the parents, he will feel inclined to receive endopsychic perceptions of his idiom and to project them into objects, as early formations of the path of desire. A child of three, receiving such a bit of idiom urge, may imagine himself swimming the crawl. This could be an endopsychic projection of a personality potential which objectifies its possibility in the image, and perhaps the eventual action, of swimming. Another child will imagine playing the piano, another playing football, etc. If all goes well, a child will develop passionate interests in objects, many of which project the child into the future. The destiny drive, then, makes use of unconscious projections of idiom potential into objects which are organized by the child and set up for true self experiencing. If so, then the urge to elaborate has the assistance of an ego capable of endopsychic projection of the figurations of idiom, imagining objects which are projections of idiom, and through the use of the actual object, the child comes into passionate expression of himself.

What are the implications of this idea of a sense of destiny in the clinical situation? In what ways can the psychoanalyst use this concept?

It should be clear that I think that one of the tasks of an analysis is to enable the analysand to come into contact with his destiny, which means the progressive articulation of his true self through many objects. The analytic process, then, becomes a procedure for the establishment and elaboration of one's idiom rather than simply the deconstruction of material or the analytic mapping of mental processes and the fate of internal objects. By introducing an element of play in my work with Jerome, I signified myself as an object available for a particular use, in order to facilitate the patient's elaboration of a part of himself that he had yet to experience.

This view of analysis holds that the patient's provision of material should at certain times be treated as if it does not as yet yield a latent content which could be found tucked away in the slips of language. In some respects, the latent content, if we think of the true self, can only be discovered through object usage, as otherwise it could not be established, and therefore could never be found.

The analyst destroys the patient's manifest texts in order to reveal unconscious meanings, and the patient destroys the analyst through that particular object usage we call transference. Each transference use of the analyst is in some respects a destruction of the analyst's true personality, and this ruthless employment of the analyst is essential to the patient's articulation of his early environment, representations of his psychic life, or elaboration of his true self through experience.

I suggest that for a good destruction of the analyst to take place, one that is not constituted out of the death instinct, but is part of the life instinct, the analyst must indicate to the patient, at the right moment, that he is ready for destruction. The 'to be destroyed' analyst has a different function – indeed is a different object – from that analyst who deconstructs the material. And I am quite sure that when I concentrate on interpreting some aspects of the material or the transference that I announce to the patient that I am the thinking or reflecting object. In some respects I would then be that object that is a mental process, part of the reflective procedure established by both patient and analyst. As the object who is somewhat playful, I am the object of play. The technical aspect of when the analyst should function differently in order to provide a different object for the patient is obviously a crucial issue, and one that makes analytic work challenging and creative.

Some analysts will immediately object to the idea that the analyst should aim to be any object for the patient. This smacks of an active technique. But one of the flaws to this kind of objection, it seems to me, is the thoughtless assumption that ordinary or classical technique is not active. We know in fact that it is. The analyst asks the patient to lie on the couch. That's an action. He remains silent and does not engage in socially conventional forms of behaviour. That's an action. He does not answer questions. These actions form part of the psychoanalytic praxis.

Part of Winnicott's (1947) conceptualization of the countertransference is that in part this amounts to an act of provision. The analyst provides the patient with his silence, his absence of socialization, his evenly hovering attentiveness. This provision elicits a certain kind of self state in the patient, one that is conducive to analysis. Within the same spirit of provision one can talk of the analyst's use of humour as provision. It is a way of announcing to the patient that the analyst is at play and in that moment the analytical situation shifts slightly from a space which potentializes reflective consideration of unconscious contents to a place that is a potential for the imaginative use of the analyst.

Changing in one's use to a patient is not, however, an applied act. The analyst has no choice. As the analysand uses the analyst, so too is the analyst affected. A funny remark inspires a humorous response in the analyst, who is used as a bearer of that which is conveyed in humour. Often a patient will diminish the analyst evoking an increased irritation in the analyst, which may eventually change the analyst into a challenging object. Jill is a case in point.

Jill

Jill had been in analysis with me for two years, and I knew from her accounts of relations with men that when she felt slighted, she would give a bloke the cold shoulder. I knew, of course, it would be my fate to be the object of such coldness, and, sure enough, this happened. Initially she would leave a session, wordless, her head virtuously erect, her movements reminiscent of Boadicea sallying forth, her gaze fixed straight ahead. This started as a Friday session phenomenon and I commented on it, saying that she was upset and cross over our relationship being interrupted by the weekend. When she would go silent, as in 'stony silent', during a Friday hour, I would say that she had just experienced the separation and that it felt awful. These comments did not enable her to talk about her state of mind other than to inspire a strange sort of strangled speech as she suffered to speak to me. 'Well, I *suppose* you could put it that way, couldn't you?' she would say, and, if I would follow up with, 'You might put it differently?' she would reply 'Pardon me?' I would repeat myself and she would say 'Possibly', or 'I don't know; you are the analyst, *aren't*

37

you?' in a witheringly sarcastic manner. In the early stages of this enactment the patient would emerge from such moods to tell me how she had been feeling, and even laugh at how awful she had been to me. But as time passed these moods increased both in frequency and duration. It was no longer organized around a weekend; it could, and eventually did, last all week – or even for ten days. Each session I would take this up as an expression of her cold fury with me that I was such a disappointing analyst, because I would not be with her all the time. She was going to eject me (as she felt cast off) to make me suffer. Sometimes an entire session would pass, and she would say nothing. At other times she would say 'You *are* right, I am going to punish you'. Occasionally with transcendental effort she would rise above me and glutted with reluctance tell me some episode from her work or life that had upset or pleased her.

We all know what it's like to get up in the morning and draw the curtains to have our first look at the day's weather. It can be a good moment of anticipation. But walking into the waiting room to greet Jill reminded me of those rather dreadful mornings in London when it had been raining and overcast continuously for six weeks, so that in drawing the curtain, one more or less knew what to expect.

I worked with a determined variation of one essential interpretation: that she felt rejected and in turn aimed to give me the cold shoulder. As abandonment by the mother was an important theme in her life, I said that she aimed for mother–me to have a dose of abandonment, a 'shared' experience that brought us closer together as victims of sorts.

After a while I actually thought to myself that I didn't think I could stand to be with this patient one moment longer. In particular I found the extremely cold and dead partings unspeakably awful, and even though I interpreted from countertransference that she was recreating an early experience of being cast off by the mother, this did not alter her self state.

Then one day, after ten minutes of her killing silence, I said, 'You know, *you* are a monster'. I said it quietly and matter of factly. She inhaled and in a kind of sepulchral cough said 'Why do you say that?' 'Because you are a monster', I replied. She said nothing and lapsed back into silence. 'I suppose', I said, 'that you are now going to be silent for the remaining twenty minutes?' She was silent. 'Well of course you intend to; I can see that', I said and then I went on: 'But you are being monstrous, and this is inhuman behaviour on your part'. At this point she clenched her fists, burst into tears of fury and said, 'I cannot help it. There is nothing I can do about it. That's all.' She reached for her handbag, fumbled about in it and produced a mighty white cloth which she blew into with extraordinary force. 'You certainly can help it', I replied. 'Well, I'm not', she said. A longer silence, the session ended, and the next day she walked ahead of me to the consulting room like the Statue of Justice irately compelled by necessity to assume human form in order to punish the more inaccessible criminals such as psychoanalysts. 'How *dare* you call me a monster!' she cried out. She went on for some minutes saying that I had no right to say something like that to her. I was meant to tell her what I thought was behind her conflicts, to help her, not to assault her like I had. I said, 'I am not sorry that I said you were a monster, because you are being one, but I do regret that it had to be said to you in that way'. Again she went into a fury, and then I said, 'Do you have any idea what it's like to sit with you day in, day out, with you an absolute ice maiden of rage? Do you? Well, let me tell you. It's dreadful. We have analysed why you do this, but I think understanding is not what you want. You insist that I suffer! Well, let me tell you, it's monstrous, and you had better do something about it if you ever expect to rid yourself of your terrible moods.' It is difficult to recreate my state of mind. I do have to emphasize that I was actually suffering, and that I had decided to combat my patient's use (abuse) of me in the transference rather than simply to interpret it.

To my surprise and relief, Jill said, 'Well, I have been very cruel to you, I know, but you have hurt me' – referring to my failure to provide her with actual love. In the months following this session, whenever she would resume a period of killing silences, I would combat her, 'Ah! The deadly silence again!' and she would leap into fury, but eventually this shifted to more aggressive encounters with the patient being counter-combative in a specific way, occasionally spelling out how something I had said, or not said, had upset her. I supported her right to 'quarrel' with me, and in my view these experiences in her analysis were important to her accomplishment of new self experiences. By quarrelling with me she engaged in reciprocal aggression with an object, an experience previously unknown to her. This illustrates another way in which an analyst's status as an object (in this instance a combative one) enables the patient to move into new self experience through the course of such use.

Jill's experiences of her primary objects, through which she could not elaborate her true self, biased her to deaden herself and others, thus identifying with her fate and imposing it in the analysis upon me. As I am a psychoanalyst, meant to have unending supplies of patience, and as Jill was a very angry and negating patient, just being herself, it was simply my bad luck that my interpretations of the patient's negative transference had no mutative effect. My professional demeanour obliged me to remain strictly analytic and patiently and calmly to analyse the negative transference, while Jill's transference intent was to turn this demeanour against myself, to turn it into a fateful attitude. To some extent, 'You are a monster', broke the customs of analysis and emerged from another part of me, perhaps expressing the need of my true self to destroy a pathological object relation, and in order to find and use those psychoanalytic objects (including the analytic process) that form my professional identity.

My destruction of the negative transference, which had already been analysed, but remained intact, enabled the analysand to use the field of analytical objects available to her. To some extent, then, this destruction of an imposed fate enabled the patient to rediscover her true self within the psychoanalytic context. If the analysand can employ the analyst to multiple effect then an analysis is destiny, as the patient uses the analyst and the analytic process to articulate the terms of their personality.

A psychoanalysis then is a means of providing different objects for the patient who uses the objects to experience and accomplish varying self states which are derivative of the idiom of the person. Such an elaboration proceeds through the use of the analyst as a transference object where usage precedes thinking and then knowing. As I have said elsewhere (Bollas, 1987), we could say that personal idiom is known but has not yet been thought and that it is part of the unthought known. So one of the features of a psychoanalysis is to think the unthought known, which is part of the core of the individual, and to do so through object usage and the drive to unfold the self through space and time.

Futures

A person who is fated, who is fundamentally interred in an internal world of self and object representations that endlessly repeat the same scenarios, has very little sense of a future that is at all different from the internal environment they carry around with them. The sense of fate is a feeling of despair to influence the course of one's life. A sense of destiny, however, is a different state, when the person feels he is moving in a personality progression that gives him a sense of steering his course. 'How amusing it is', writes Alice James (1979), 'to see the fixed mosaic of one's little destiny being filled out by tiny blocks of events – the enchainment of minute consequences with the illusion of choice weathering it all.' Such an enchainment also forms a basis for the subject's projection of himself in the future. Any person who is partly living from the true self will project idiom possibilities into the future, and I shall term such projections 'futures'. If we can say of most people that they have memories, so too they have futures. Of course this term is popular in economic theory. When a person buys a future, he invests in the future as favourable to his well-being. Interestingly, Freud referred to the organizations of futures in his paper on 'The uncanny' (1919): 'There are also all the unfulfilled but possible futures to which we still like to cling in phantasy, all the strivings of the ego which adverse external circumstances have crushed, and all our suppressed acts of volitions which nourish in us the illusion of Free Will' (p. 236). People who have a sense of destiny also invest psychically in the future. This involves a certain necessary ruthlessness and creative destructiveness, of the past and the present, in order to seek conditions necessary for futures.

For example, let us think of the selection of a partner. Let us imagine that I am young again and single. I see a woman whom I like and enjoy knowing, but I do not find her sexually attractive. Now let us say that a question emerges: 'Should I marry her?' What right have I to refuse to do this if we add that this person would like to marry me? Now let us add that if I do not marry this person, she will feel terribly upset by my refusal. Should I not marry her, because I know her to be a very decent, intelligent, and creative person? Well, of course, we know that some people would marry under these conditions and, indeed, it is one of the interesting facts of life that in the course of the marriage the man might become sexually attracted to the woman. Or we know that he might marry out of unconscious reparative needs. But I am referring to the essential ruthlessness that is a factor in the refusal to marry, a ruthlessness that in effect amounts to the following statement, 'No, I am not going to marry you, because I am not sexually attracted to you'.

The choice of partner, of vocation, of city or country, can be made for similarly ruthless reasons – an essential ruthlessness, which is part of the destiny drive. There is an urge to invest in futures which to the true self are potential spaces not yet immediately at hand. Many people who live from the true self, relatively unhindered by conflict, may have a sense of destiny which generates futures, or visions of the self in a temporal progression beyond the present. That 'inner sense' that people rely upon to choose an object is a sense of destiny, and some individuals may root about amongst present objects in order to select a suitable object to fulfil a future. Imagine that I have a sense of the man I feel myself to be, and that this self is contingent upon my choice of partner. If I choose the right partner who knows the essence of me, then I shall be freer to be my self than otherwise might be the case. Or imagine I am at university, and I have a choice: do I study psychology, literature, history, or social anthropology? These disciplines will, to some extent, overlap. But as I imagine myself in the future, working in these areas, which one do I feel to be the evolution of my idiom? Where shall I find experiences of myself?

The person who lives from this inner sense of destiny will have an intuitive knowledge of object choice based on the need to express the idiom of the true self, and will in turn have imaginary objects (futures) that are visions of potential use. Such objects, yet to be met, nonetheless collect interest, as the subject will explore objects related to this future object, and perhaps acquire a 'skill' that is meanwhile quite useful and eventually of further use in the time to come. One of my children, for example, developed a passion for BMX bicycles. He decorated his bicycle handsomely, tinkered with it endlessly, and drove it mercilessly. It was clear to him that although it was a bicycle, it was also an intermediate object that was intrinsically linked to a future. In this respect, it was also a car. Indeed, its decorations, his freely supplied sound effects, his fascination with its speed, meant that he was really driving a Porsche. Present objects are often pregnant with futures and a person who has an inner sense of his or her destiny will, if conditions present, choose objects that facilitate access to futures.

A person who feels fated may imagine futures that carry the weight of despair. Instead of feeling the energy of a destiny drive and of 'possessing' futures which nourish the person in the present and creatively serve to explore pathways for potential travel (through object use), the fated person only projects the oracular. A glimpse into the future, a vision from fate, only echoes the voice of the mother, the father, or the socio-cultural context which oppresses the self. There is, then, no wish to call up futures, as the person does not wish to evoke painful memories. Indeed we can speak of the repression of futures, in the same way as we speak of the repression of memories. If they contain too much distress, futures are as liable to be repressed as painful memories.

The loss of futures for a child is a very particular kind of loss. A simple and obvious example is the child who, when losing a parent, loses the future relation to the object. Each child unconsciously invests in the parent as a future object, and has an unconscious sense of the potential uses of the object throughout development, a use that is inextricably linked to the elaboration of the true self. Thus the loss of a parent forecloses, in some respects, the use of the parental object, the articulation of self via the object, and therefore those futures that derive from the successful use of objects. A sense of fate, the projection of the present terms into the future, will prevail, and the drive to fulfil one's destiny, to drive the true self into being and relating, will not be accomplished.

What is that grief that occurs when a child or adolescent loses futures? In a certain respect it is a loss of potential selves, a mourning for what could have been and now will not be. The acute anguish, if not rage, of such a person is extraordinary – and understandable. Rage over being fated, rather than destined, may result in the negative celebration of fatedness, as in *Richard III*, when Richard tries to make his fate into a destiny by assuming a pseudo-joyful 'control' over his future by being monstrous. But for those of us who watch or read the play, his futures are projected forms of grief and encapsulated states of pain.

It may be an essential part of analytic work to help a patient transform fatedness into destiny and to gain futures. Nancy comes to mind.

Nancy

Nancy is an intelligent, thoughtful, punkish young woman who contacted me for analysis, or, rather, who used a friend to contact me. A colleague called me and said somewhat apologetically that his son knew a young woman who was training to be a solicitor and who wanted analysis. Would I give a consultation? I said I would be pleased to do so. My colleague paused and then said somewhat ill at ease, 'Well, I should tell you that she can be rather difficult'. He said that Nancy had expressed interest in seeing me (she knew of me through the analyst's son) but had said she had 'no idea' when or if she would ever contact me. Would it be possible for me to remember her name and see her in the future, even if I did not at that time have a vacancy? I agreed.

Over a year went by, and one day a very charming voice on the phone said, 'Is this *Christopher* Bollas?' in a way that I quite liked my name being used. 'This is Nancy X. You won't know me but ...' and she narrated the account of her contact with my colleague. I said, 'Yes, I do remember. I have been expecting to hear from you.' We set a time for her to come and see me.

I will not describe the first meeting, except to say that I found her mischievous and depressed at the same time. She said she wanted to begin analysis but could only come at hours completely determined by her, changing week to week, but she would call me each day to tell me when she would come. I was astonished that she seemed to be serious, and, after saying that this was impossible, I stressed that she seemed determined to put me in a situation where it would appear that I had failed her. We parted, and another fifteen months passed before I saw her again.

The analysis did eventually begin and was interesting and worthwhile – for both of us. I will only focus on one element – the element of fate. For Nancy had, as I had seen, this remarkable knack of making extraordinarily arbitrary and silly statements which sealed actions. I learned about this from her narration of life with her boyfriend. While they were both relaxing in the living room, Nancy would say, 'We are going to the opera!' This would come completely out of the blue. She did not say, 'I would like to go to the opera', or indicate that it was a wish. She said it as if announcing the evening's fate. This sudden oracular voice typified her in other relations as well and would have seriously jeopardized her career had she not been in some ways remarkably responsible when working on a task. She was only this way with colleagues in a social situation, and the rest of the time she had an impish smile playing across her face: a reminder that she could and would announce sudden action that would alter the course of life at any moment.

Once I knew of Nancy's early life, it was not difficult to understand this characteristic, for her parents had treated her similarly. They periodically intervened fatefully in her life by commanding her (and one another) into certain drastically alternative actions, such as suddenly changing schools, clothing styles, houses, friends, or vacations. Everything was topsy-turvy. What would mother or father declare next? And these declarations were fateful, as they directly affected the life of the children, who found themselves continuously cast into new situations.

At the beginning of her analysis, Nancy simply enacted the familiar environment, but in time she 'calmed down'. From this position, it was possible for us to listen to her own wishes and for her to grasp that wishing could be an internally fruitful act. She had never known what she had wanted to do. For some time she leapt into outrage whenever I made an interpretation that felt to her like an oracle. I very carefully indicated how I associated to what she said, thus helping to derive our future from her comments. In this respect, we can see how ordinary analytic attentiveness, supplemented by the analyst's associative comments, facilitates the right of the patient to live from the core of the self, and for the destiny of associations in the analytic hour to be determined from and by the true self.

On reflection, Nancy's impulsive announcements were somewhere between fateful commandments and destined actions. An impulse could be seen as an expression of true self movement, so when Nancy declared 'We are going to the opera', she was partly espousing a future to give course to an element needing some particular experience at that moment. But Nancy's seeming spontaneity always occurred in relation to, and at the immediate cost of, the other, for whom her apparent destiny was the other's fate. In parodying the destiny drive in this way, I think Nancy demonstrated her experience of parents who followed their destinies at the cumulative expense of their children. The other then had to carry the burden of the self's action.

If there is a ruthlessness essential to object selection and use, such an element should obviously not become a rationale for thoughtless and egocentric action at the dynamic cost to the other. A dynamic cost is an act committed by the subject that is intrinsically destructive to the other and recurs, if not behaviourally, then intrapsychically. If Jack is at a party, sees Betty whom he courts, Mary may feel disappointed, but Jack's ruthless choice (acting only for himself) will not cause Mary dynamic harm. If, however, Jack initially courts Mary, then 'chucks' her upon seeing Betty, this is somewhat harmful. Some form of reparative work may be essential to help Mary deal with the after-effects of such an experience, as Jack has elicited her desire, engaged himself with her, then discarded her. He has been in dynamic relation to her.

Nonetheless, we often act out of self-interest, in a form of ruthlessness that we feel to be essential to the evolution of our idiom. And to varied extents, this will affect the other. As an undergraduate I studied history, and several of my professors wanted me to continue with graduate studies in that field. I chose instead to study English literature. This disappointed my professors, but I made my choice because I knew I could find more of what I was searching for through literary studies. To my mind, this is ruthlessness of a non-dynamic kind, as it is a form of object selection which does not have destruction either as its aim or as its primary effect.

Of course, we are always involved in necessary compromises between our inner drive to articulate our idiom through experiences of objects and the contexts in which we live. The internal world is the arena in which the claims of the drive and the context of our lives are objectified, particularly when the needs of the other suggest to us the necessity to restrict, delay, displace, or transform a destiny aim.

In the previous chapter I have argued that imaginative projections of true self idiom are likely, and I have used Freud's theory of endopsychic perception to argue this. I think we project our idiom into imaginary objects which then partly serve as precursors of more direct lived experience. There is an imaginative forerunner of true self action, although I think imaginative acts are already articulations of one's idiom, as the subject expresses very precise idiom features through the choice and use of imaginary objects.

In this respect, then, the dream is an even more unique event than we already know it to be. For in this special place the subject partly creates the object of his future. Is this an argument for the prophetic character of dreams? In a way, yes. 'By picturing our wishes as fulfilled', Freud wrote, 'dreams are after all leading us into the future' (1900, p. 621). Although he rightly dismissed the idea that the subject foretells the future through the work of a special part of the mind, Freud believed that as the past recreates itself in the future, the dreamer can, to an extent, correctly foretell such futures. 'Who could deny that wishes are predominantly turned towards the future?' he asks.

We may agree with Freud that a dreamer creates his future insofar as it is determined by a past, but we may add that the dream also constitutes a fictional forerunner of reality, in which the idiom of the self is played. My stress is less on the repetition of past events, than it is on a prior knowledge coming into thought through the formation of dream thoughts as an early 'playing about' with reality before the imaginary becomes the actual.

At the very least, then, the dream creates futures, visions of the self in transformed states that are nonetheless articulations of the individual's unique person. It does not simply generate futures, it is vital to the subject's formation of the future. It is where some futures are hatched. It is the origin of vision, the place where the subject plays with objects, moving through potential patterns, setting up fields of imagined persons, places, selves and events – to be there as potential actuals for future use. If we think of this in Bion's terms, when the dream produces thoughts, alpha funcion transforms idiom potential into imaginary realizations, converting personality preconceptions into imaginary realizations.

The destiny of any of us then is more than slightly determined in advance. A *déjà vu*, the sense of having lived precisely this event before, may be an existential signature of the recurring resonance between the dream and the future, as some of our action experiences will have been dreamt before.

'The greatest things that man has done, he owes to the painful sense of incompleteness of his destiny' muses Madame de Staël (1985). This incompleteness that we must all endure is a special sense of loss, as each of us is only ever a part subject, an incomplete sample of our potential. But we are mercifully free of the ideal of completion. As it has never been accomplished, it does not form a part of our ordinary ego ideals, and many of the differing theologies of an after-life accept the impossibility of completion on earth while posing different places (a heaven) or forms (reincarnation) where presumably we continue to elaborate our potential. But we don't. We are stopped by our deaths and usually long before then – in what we modestly phrase a mid-life crisis – we have an inkling of how we shall not be destined after all to fulfil our urge to be fully present in our own existence.

The Fashioning of a Lifetime

In the course of a day, a week, a year, or a lifetime we are engaged in successive selections of objects, each of which suits us at the moment, 'provides' us with a certain kind of experience, and, as our choice, may serve to articulate our idiom, recall some earlier historical situation, or foreclose true self articulation.

In the last week I have read certain books. Why have I read what I have? Why have I rejected certain possibilities? When I listen to a record why do I select certain pieces of music and reject others? When I go for a walk, where do I go? When I seek a night out, which form of entertainment do I choose? Do not these choices provide textures of self experience that release me to articulate some idiom move on my part?

Sometimes we are conscious of why we choose what we do. More often than not, however, we choose our objects because we seek the experience potential of the choice. We need the object to release our self into expression. And now and then we will be quite transformed by the uncanny wedding of our idiom and an object, meeting up at just the right time. One late afternoon in the summer of 1972, I heard a performance of one of Hindemith's viola sonatas in a small church in New England. It immediately served to process a feature of my idiom, and this occasion sponsored vivid and intense feelings and ideas which lifted me into the next moments of my life. Shall we ever have the means to analyse that? Why that particular work?

When we have lived all there is of our lifetime, our families and friends will at some point look through and sort out what we call 'personal effects'. What an interesting way to describe what we leave behind. Effects. Articles of use? What I have caused to come into my existence as expressions of the very particular life I have lived? Why not borrow this ceremonial phrase and apply it to living? What are my personal effects? Where are they? As psychoanalysts we have, of course, to include the persons we affect and what we create in them of ourself and former others. Aside from this psychological establishment, we create a field of objects which serve to express our idiom and are its signature. Each of us establishes a private culture, and personal effects are those cultural objects we generate.

In health the true self continuously establishes its idiom and the fashioning of a life is the work of the destiny drive, as our urge to elaborate this idiom partly results in our creation of personal effects. As the psychoanalyst tills away, interpreting the roots of free association, identifying the branches of transference expression and reconstructing the family trees in a patient's life, he must find some way to catch glimpses of the forest. Does he have a point of view that enables him to see the analysand's culture? If he is useful as a multiple object, if his presence is the object of the patient's true self, then he will, in time, carry many of the patient's personal effects, and the destiny of the analysand will have been partly fulfilled: to establish a cultural life from the idiom of the true self.

3

Off the Wall

Countertransference theory serves an increasingly important function in the therapeutic community, as it allows the psychoanalyst to talk about his own emotional reality, mental processes, and self states as they exist in his work with patients. Freud led the way in *The Interpretation of Dreams* when he spoke about himself in what we refer to as his self analysis. Unfortunately, though, this very important part of the psychoanalytical situation – the self-analytical element – has been fixed as an historical figuration of Freud's. Occasional references have been made in the literature since Freud about the necessity for practising analysts to continue with a self analysis, but the analytic community has made comparatively little effort to evolve and use that voice that Freud established in his writings – a voice that speaks of the person's experience as both subject and object. There are some notable exceptions.

The Psychoanalyst as Subject

I am most familiar with the efforts of English psychoanalysts to represent themselves in the literature as a subject. Winnicott found a way to write about himself. Bion, inscrutable yet evocative, private yet publicly adept, rigorously innocent and shrewdly analytic, comes to mind as a most courageous leader in the evolution of the analyst as subject. Think of his remarkable work *A Memoir of the Future* (1975), a fantastic autobiography, impossible to believe and yet strangely true to psychic life. In *The Hands of the Living God* (1988), Marion Milner wrote about herself in a way which enables the reader to participate in her life with Susan. Certainly Theodore Reik (1956) found language for his own inner experiences, and Harold Searles (1965) has established a narrative voice which enables the reader to know him, not simply as the analyst–interpreter, but as a subject in the total field of analysis.

There is something of a collective simultaneity of commitment amongst psychoanalysts in many different parts of the world to include the analyst's frame of mind as a valued source of information and to write in such a way as to inform the reader of this private use. I refer especially to the writings of McDougall (1985), Symington (1983), Coltart (1986), Ehrenberg (1984), Stewart (1985), Klauber (1981), Feiner (1979), Giovacchini (1979), Rosenfeld (1987), Joseph (1982), Pedder (1976), Limentani (1981), King (1978), and Little (1981).

Of course we all know how embarrassing and irritating it can be when a colleague, in the name of scientific self-scrutiny, or humanist self-knowledge, promotes a 'confessional voice' to bear his disclosure of mind, affect, and self in work with a patient. I know that we have all been in such a position, where we are compelled to listen to a clinician's intercourse with honesty, giving birth to a revelatory issue that none of us believes. Any of us can, under certain conditions, compel ourself to disclose to our colleagues our inner state of mind in work with a patient. But in some situations this amounts to an abreactive abortion of psychic states, inspiring in the audience a kind of annoyance over the falseness of such a presentation. I did not know Winnicott, but I have heard from his many colleagues that to read him is like being with him. He is there in his prose. I attended Bion's seminars, and I know that reading his work is strikingly similar to being with him. And Marion Milner, who is possessed of a very rare gift indeed, represents her self in her writing.

When we objectify our self, either in that intermittent inner subvocal dialogue that is the opera of our internal world, or when we speak to the other about our self, we stand at some slight remove from this self that we are and we address this object that is our self. Freud did this in his self analysis and my view is that such a procedure, of establishing a dialogue with one's self, is a feature of what we could term subject relations theory. Subject relations theory refers to the complex field of relations any one person has to himself (and from himself) as an individual. Finding a way to be a subject, in oral or written discourse, means finding a way to express one's inner status in the moment, unhindered by the knowledge that no such subjective state shall ever escape the problematics of unconscious context.

It is my view that the successful establishment of the analyst as a subject in the field of psychoanalysis, whether this is accomplished in prose, or, as I will discuss shortly, in clinical work with a patient, depends on the integrity of the analyst's relation to his own subjectivity. This evolution of the self-analytic element, into prose or interpretive work with patients, is a discipline that is achieved only by rigorous work. The patient or the reading public should be able to link the analyst's narrative of his subjectivity to the analyst's person. This compatibility of idioms (person and narrative) authorizes the value of the self-analytic element and differentiates it from a seduction. A disclosure of mental content, psychic process, emotional reality, or self state (whether in writings or in sessions) that is congruent with the person of the analyst is unlikely to be an artifice or a seduction. There must be integrity to the self-analytic process for it to be of use to us, either as patients or as analysts reading someone's writings. It is this discipline and integrity which, I think, lead us to celebrate the written works of persons such as Milner, Winnicott, Bion, and Searles, because we sense the authenticity of their use of self as an object in the analytic field.

Although I shall discuss the clinical uses of the analyst's experiences as subject in the analytical field shortly, my present intent is to address the function of the analyst's reports to his colleagues. (How can we develop a narrative that will account for our psychic presence in the analytical situation?) While it is important to know what interpretation an analyst gives to his patient, in the name of psychoanalysis, it is equally interesting to know what he has thought of saying, but withheld. In the course of any session that is reported, what wayward thoughts, fantasies, or images have crossed the analyst's mind? How does his imaginative conception of the patient change? This is slightly different from wondering what his object representations of the patient are, as an imaginative conception suggests an intersubjective process that heeds the laws of such mutual unconscious communication. As the patient narrates his life (let us say, the details of his previous day's encounters), how does the analyst imagine the patient as a participant in history? If a patient tells me about visiting a friend, of how this friend criticizes the patient for something, and of how the patient responded to this criticism, do I simply identify with the patient, experiencing the friend as critical? Or do I imagine the encounter differently? Do I identify with the friend and agree with his criticism of the patient? Do I accept the narrative at least as a process if not the content, reasonably at peace with simply listening, or does an objection occur to me, stopping me from simply listening, moving me to an interrogative position, or into an affective response to the narrative?

Off the Wall

What are the origins of an interpretation? Some interpretations might be quite obvious to the patient and analyst (and to colleagues hearing it), but much of our work involves exploring issues that are not clear. What is the basis of a particular emphasis in our questions to a patient? Why do I select a detail from the narrative and exclude other factors? Why do I respond to a patient's request for a response and yet at other times remain silent? I can, of course, add many such questions, but I will have done my work if it is clear that I want to have greater access to the analyst's inner world in considering the practices of psychoanalysis and the theories that derive from these practices.

I must begin with a question – one that I have asked myself these last months. As I enjoy something of a sabbatical from intensive psychoanalytical work, reflecting on a now defined previous period of some ten years of psychoanalytic practice, I ask myself, 'Where were you?' No answer springs immediately to mind. Where have I been?

Superficially, I have lived a more or less ten-hour clinical day in a rather comfortable room which was part of my home in London. I could say that I have been living a particular kind of life in that room. Is it different from other rooms? I think it is. Unlike my living room, or my study, or any place where I spend a fair amount of time, the analytic space is somewhere between physical and psychical reality. The room changes each day. It changes from hour to hour. It has a different feel from patient to patient. There are also periods in the day that give this room a certain definition. The house changes slightly and thus effects the analytic room. If the children are away at school, and I am absolutely assured there will be no noise, then I am more at rest than I am when they are either just going off to school or coming back. They tend to bang the front door shut in such a manner as to slightly shake the house. And, of course, every morning at 8.15 I tend to wait for the house to shake.

But the room has a curious way of coming to mind when I ask myself where I have been. I have been in that room, and it is a space somewhere between the physical and the psychic. But if I approach the question from a very different angle and remind myself that I was once something of an athlete, and at another time a university scholar, and if I recall running the 400 metres and remember teaching Shakespeare, then armed with these memories, how do I proceed to say what the act of psychoanalysis is? The mind boggles.

I remember escorting people into the consulting room. But after years of knowing the same person so intensively, I'm not sure it's accurate to say that it is quite the same thing any more as escorting a person into the consulting room. I don't think the concept 'person' quite describes what that moment is like. I can recall escorting a particularly difficult woman into the room who was enmeshed in a negative transference. Inviting her into the room was more akin to opening the door to the furies. It amounted to a transportation of mental elements. Another patient who went through a very severe depression was so adept at conveying this mood that it felt as if I were physically lifting him into the room. Another patient always entered the room like an eager actor rushing on to the stage, the understudy's moment; I usually felt momentarily awkward until I sat down. I suppose I was then more comfortably situated in that position – as audience – that I was meant to occupy.

Sometimes I would sit down, in the classical place, simply pleased to be able to listen and concentrate. At other moments, I would sit down in order to be comforted by my chair, protected from the predictable battle that would ensue. I can recall a time when a patient, towards the end of her analysis and by then very much better, enabled me to sit in my chair for the fun of it. Regrettably there were times when I think I must have approached my position like someone heading toward the rack: fifty minutes of torture!

While sitting in my chair, out of the patient's view, I would look at different objects in my visual field and in different ways. Is it possible that the analyst's visual experience of his object world is unconsciously co-ordinate with the patient's discourse and transference usage of the analyst? If only we could find a way to discover the logical paradigms of patient–analyst interaction. I would often look at a nice long off-white wall opposite me. During the course of the day's journey the wall would register the light in subtle ways and this was enhanced by the fact that the surface was uneven, enabling it to have a mixed media potential. I would gaze at the wall, often invited by the figurations of light, or I would look into it as a material eternity, with different patients over different periods of time for, I am sure, varying reasons. Although I have paintings, ceramics, oriental rugs, and other objects in my visual field, I feel confident that certain of my interpretations were, to coin a phrase, 'off the wall'.

I saw a schizophrenic woman in analysis. She spoke infrequently, and after a very long time working with her, when the fabric of coherent thought faded and I felt rather lost, I was aware that when I listened to her I always looked at the different patterns of light on the wall, or out the window at cloud formations, but I rarely 'travelled' about the room looking at the space's 'internal' objects. I believe, on reflection, that my visual orientations metaphorized my state of mind. I could not focus on this patient's internal objects, nor on the hard direct objects in the room. I expect that when I looked at the complex, visually articulate patterns on the rug this was a different psychological act from when I was lost in the wall. And sometimes I would look at my shoes, or my torso, or my hands. Why? Where was I? Well, when I looked at my watch, at least I could answer that question!

And where was I during those hundreds of hours listening to the patient talking to me or undergoing a particular articulation as the transference object? I am reminded of Paula Heimann's classic formulation of the transference. We must ask who is speaking, to whom, about what, and why at that moment. She emphasized that the object of the address, the content, and the motivation could change many times in any one session. The patient could begin as mother speaking to the analyst as an adolescent, then recall an adolescent regression to earlier child states and swiftly alter the speaking voice to that of a mother addressing a small child analyst, then move to being the small child addressing the analyst mother, who might subtly change into the father, eliciting in the analysand a different child voice. Later, Bion suggested that we could not simply conceptualize this process according to whole persons or even parts of whole persons, and that it would be more accurate to speak of elements of the mind addressing one another. But as I look back on my work to wonder where I was and to think about the origins of interpretation, I recall that extraordinary experience of not knowing what analysis was and yet of being the analyst. Although I did upbraid myself now and then for not knowing what an analyst was, I developed an increasing respect for this position and over time regarded it as an important, indeed essential, feature to being a psychoanalyst. Does this mean being someone who does not know his own being? To some extent I think it does, and certainly Bion (1970) has said as much. I believe I am addressing that mental frame of mind he described when talking about the analyst's responsibility to be without memory or desire; I also think this absence of knowing is perhaps true of that psychic state accomplished by evenly hovering attentiveness. After all, if we are evenly hovering ten hours a day for tens of thousands of hours in our analytic lifetime, it's fair enough to think that our sense of our being as an analyst will be rather odd.

The Sources of Interpretation

Where did my interpretations come from? I think I never knew. I do not mean that I never knew what I thought. Like all analysts, I had an idea of what I thought the patient meant, and I would put it to him for consideration. When making a reconstructive interpretation, I would take care to put the construction in simple and basic terms, and I did so believing that my formulation was correct. But that does not address the problem of the origins of an interpretation. I knew what I thought, but I did not know why I had that particular idea (and not several other plausible ones) at that moment. However, I have said that this not knowing is essential to analytic practice, which leads me to wonder if my interpretations came from that life the patient created for us. Each analysand uses us as object: we are guided, given shape. One moment we are moved into this person's adolescent position, later his infant state. Another moment we are being shaped into the father or aspects of the mother. Sometimes we are utilized for our mental functioning, and it's more pertinent to say we are used as a function of an element of psyche. No doubt some of my interpretations came from my interior mood, biasing me toward the selection of content and sponsoring a certain emphasis I gave to my comments. I am not saying that my interpretations are the final evolution of the patient's projective identifications, but I do think that my interpretations are inseparable from the patient's use of me in the transference. I do not believe there is such a thing as interpretive neutrality or a surgical stance that allows one a mood of emotional coldness, as Freud suggests. What I think of saying to this particular patient is inseparable from the fact that it is this patient to whom I deliver this comment. What I say may sound like other comments delivered to other patients, but it is not the same.

I am inclined to say something ridiculous in order to push myself further toward answering this question: Where do interpretations come from? Well, I shall begin with a sane answer. They come from our 'understanding' of the meaning implicit in the patient's discourse. Freud wrote of identifying nodal points. Or we can ask ourselves in what way the patient's speech metaphorizes the transference. Well, we have many models for organizing the analytical material, but I do not think such frames of reference process all that is conveyed.

For example, it came to my attention one day that while with a particular patient I was holding my breath. I was not breathing properly. I was tense and felt all bunched up inside. On further consideration I realized that much of my interpretive work had come from my bunched-up soma. If an instinct is a demand upon the mind for work, for psychical representation, the patient I was with used psychical representations to make a demand on my soma for unwork. And we can wonder where those interpretations, prior to this understanding, came from. I would have to say partly from a creature (myself) that was only just breathing and all bunched up. Hardly a good medium for interpreting.

I am sure, however, that many interpretations with certain patients originate from our soma. I may ache from psychic pain affecting soma, and my interpretation will come from there – the ache. Or a patient may be so overwhelming, my anxiety so high, that I am more a creature of my respiratory system, so that some interpretations will evolve out of this somatic distress. And of course, now and then we encounter a patient who inspires erotic wishes in us – they affect our soma – and interpretive work will emerge from the struggle with that somatic registration. It is well to bear in mind that often a patient's instinctual drives seek a route to mental representation through the analyst's soma, given that the patient trusts the reliable link between analyst's soma and psyche.

But I return to the wall. Some of my interpretations seem to have come from there. I can remember the occasions when I would gaze at a particular pattern of light on the wall, which I dwelt on while listening to the patient. The effort to form an interpretation seemed to emerge from a visual place. (How different this is from interpretations that seem to spring from the auditory, in response to the patient's phonemics.) Is it possible that in 'gathering' an interpretation off the wall, I am creating a comment out of the blankness of the screen, rather than linking up signifiers latent in the word presentations? Does the pattern of light serve as an area I can go to with this patient at this moment to serve as a potential space for my comment? Sometimes the shaded and blended play of light on the wall serves as a point of inspiration, rather than the literary critique of signifier–signified, or the objectification of deep subjectivity which is part of the effort to give voice to the countertransference. Is the mental origin of this interpretation significantly different from somatic, auditory, and hermeneutic processings of a patient's being, relating, and signifying?

I seem to be saying that analysts are mediums for the psychosomatic processing of the patient's psyche-soma. And that we 'find' different patients in different locations depending on how we are unconsciously invited to process them. I may be working with someone in my soma – in the stomach, the back, or in my respiratory system. I may be considering someone on the wall, in a cloud, or somewhere in the carpet. I may textualize a patient's discourse into a phonemic script, listening to the punctuation of the unconscious.

Interpretation, then, involves the analyst in a transformation of the patient's use of the analyst-medium, a countertransference into meaning and language. Where are we when we make an interpretation? Where have I been with different patients at different times? Of course, I do not think that the content of a comment necessarily has any reference to its origin, but I do suggest that we work from or with different phenomena in the mulling over of our life with the patient just prior to a comment. I may be listening to the patient but visually intent upon looking at patterns of light on the wall. Or I may be lost in memory of a previous session. Or I may be amidst an inner body state which seems to be the primary point of perspective. The point of view does not always determine the interpretation. It is an early feature of the interpretation's status as it metaphorizes the analyst's state of mind and self at that moment.

Indeed, in the analysis of severely disturbed patients I think all analysts who are free of reassuring constraints of a particular dogma of practice (i.e., an applied psychoanalysis) have a recurring experience of no longer knowing what psychoanalysis is. Winnicott claims that he often made interpretations to inform the patients of the limits of his knowledge. But I am quite sure we make comments to hear the voice of reason amidst a most confusing situation. To some extent, we speak to the analysand to work through the unprocessed situation that confronts us. We work upon or within our self, aiming to transform our inner state, to place ourselves in a position to make an interpretation. Much of the therapeutic work of a psychoanalysis takes place entirely within the psychoanalyst as he processes his own inner turmoil, or useless ignorance, or ineffective remove, etc., in order to address the patient.

Some years ago a woman of twenty-two came to intensive therapy referred by her general practitioner. For the first three weeks she politely, and at times coyly, informed me of her life history. Then one day she came to her session, sat motionless in her chair, stared straight ahead, and said nothing. In the previous hour she had become tearful when discussing her father who had died suddenly several years before. I said that perhaps she had found remembering him sad and upsetting. She remained utterly and eerily silent. In fact she said nothing for the next ten months of her three times weekly therapy. For some time I endeavoured to hazard guesses about what was occurring to her. About a month after the onset of her silence she would occasionally rock back and forth in her chair. Then some weeks after that she gripped her left forearm with her right hand, placed between her legs, stooped over slightly, and moving her body back and forth, rocked her arm in an independent motion. Whenever I commented, she would immediately stop her rocking, stare at me intensely for a few seconds, then drop her head which would be enveloped by her very long hair. I shall not discuss those interpretations and inquiries I made. I did discuss the situation with colleagues, and I received a considerable range of views from ordinary hysteric to borderline, to catatonic schizophrenic. None of this helped me at all.

Interestingly enough, however, I did not feel greatly persecuted by this very long silence. I worked in a small under-used psychotherapy centre in central London. We had very few patients, and I really had nothing else to do with my time.

I also liked the looks of this woman. She was from the Far East and strangely beautiful. To be with her was an odd experience, but not distinctly unpleasant, and after a few months I would wander off wherever my mind would take me. Then on a lovely May day I said to her, speaking to myself out loud, 'You look like a young woman sitting on a park bench', and the patient laughed. It was from this point that she resumed talking, and after some years of psychotherapy embarked on a fruitful analysis with me.

Perhaps because I was so relieved by her resumption of speech, or perhaps because she also flooded me with information, I was not immediately aware of why I spoke and of why she replied. Where had my comment come from?

Every session this woman arrived in the very same brown paisley dress with black shoes. I didn't know whether she had additional clothes, but certainly this was what she wore to therapy. I became quite accustomed to her 'habit', to its absolute regularity. Indeed, it seemed apt, almost helpful, to that curiously pleasing meditation that occurred between us. But on the day of my comment she wore a different outfit: a flowery skirt and a white blouse. Same shoes. And I did not notice this! At least not consciously. But if we think of this act as a cue to the therapist (this was before my analytic training), then my freedom to talk out loud was perhaps sponsored by her change of habit. Of course I have had many occasions to think about this period of her therapy/analysis, and one feature is striking: that she needed a long, benign, undirected thoughtfulness on my part. She needed me to find and use those internal resources within myself, before she would make use of me. (At a later stage the analysis was stormy and intense.)

Knowing and Not Knowing

But where does this leave us? Do I conclude that we really do not know why we say what we do at any given moment to a particular patient? Does this not suggest that we are profoundly lacking in any expertise? After all, how is this not knowing any different from any other person's not knowing in the patient's life? In the United States of America, where many people sue at the drop of a hat, psychoanalysts might live in dread of a patient bringing a court action on the basis that his psychoanalyst doesn't know what he is doing. After all, other mental health professionals, armed with their diagnostic manual – the DSM III – can practise with more certainty.

To me this not knowing is an accomplishment. I am certain that it has taken me years of experience as an analyst to value this frame of mind and to know it for what it is – a necessary condition for the creation of a potential space, an inner analytic screen that we sustain and which registers the patient's idiom. The patient's registration of idiom, an in-forming not only of an instinctual derivative, but the force of true self, and the scripts of self and other, can only be established through my not knowing. Interpretation does not emerge from the patient or from myself. As Freud said, it is a dialect(ic) of two unconscious systems, and each interpretive act acknowledges this movement of patient to analyst, of analyst to patient.

Of course each analysand learns a great deal about himself through the contents of interpretation, whether that is the elucidation of a constellation of memories that are de-repressed or whether it is an enhanced understanding of the nature of certain mental processes. I believe, however, that those analysands who have truly changed very deeply are the ones who have 'grasped' the analytic sensibility, who have found that freedom that emerges with a particular kind of not knowing that is essential to progressive registrations of the self and incremental intimacy with the other. It amounts to a kind of pleasure. A pleasure in the formation of potential space, as from this discipline – essential to the life of the subject – the person can entertain ideas and feelings that arrive with the integrity of conviction.

Of course there is an inevitable tension between the analyst's urge to know and the essentials of not knowing. I am certain that my most common error as an analyst occurs when, after working with a person for some time, I have organized the individual into a set of interpretive references, yielding up in each session, one or another of ten or fifteen by now fairly routine and predictable interpretations. However, there are moments in the course of an analysis where I think it is quite right that the analyst, in working through a particular interpretation with a patient, will have to repeat himself, with variation, many times. It is important to 'hold one's ground' as we say in England – a faint refrain from a colonial past. But I am not happy with myself or my colleagues when we praise ourselves too much for our refusal to give in, for our moral upholding of the analytic stance, for our trenchant determination to interpret in the transference and not give up. It is precisely this element in us psychoanalysts that Winnicott, Bion, and Lacan have turned away from. Each analyst who comes to know his patient through a coherent analytical understanding of the patient must unknow him.

This unknowing process, perhaps akin to the concept of unbinding (see Green, 1987), is essential to any further generative knowing, and to any further symbolically complex binding. Unknowing is essential to the creation and (internal) maintenance of the interior analytic screen. That which has been known after a while must be assumed to be still available to both patient and analyst as they rid themselves of such organization of the unconscious in order to receive new unconscious communications, made possible through unknowing. In my view, this establishes something of an essential dialectic, one that I think is at the heart of creativity in living, a dialectic between knowing (organizing, seeing, cohering) and unknowing (loosening, not perceiving). I believe that those analytic theoreticians who argue that the self is an invariant, and the knowing of the self is essential to an analysis, and those who take the opposing view that the self is an illusion, an entrapment of the subject in the fields of the imaginary, are both correct. The one is indispensable to the other. Were we simply to be impressed by the invariant core that we were and to split off the unconscious as an interesting but somewhat distant element, we would create an imbalance in the equations of the dialectic. If we take the view that the self is a somewhat feeble illusion concealing from us the ineffable inscrutability of the unconscious, then we err in another direction.

How do we make use of this dialectic? What does this have to do with that place where I have been as an analyst and with the origins of interpretation?

The Dialectics of Difference

To some extent, the above is a plea for a slightly different emphasis in the practice of analysis. We need to bring more of the analytic sensibility into our work with our patients. It is inconsistent with this sensibility for the clinician simply to interpret to the patient in whatever way (calmly, diligently, for example). However correct one feels at any moment with an analysand, it is inconsistent with the entire nature of the psychoanalytic accomplishment for the analyst only to tell the patient what the unconscious meaning of his communication is, whether it is to reconstruct the past or to interpret in the here and now transference. Because at any one moment, regardless of how certain we feel, of how passionately we hold a view, or of how correct we indeed are, such certainty is the function of our knowing, but the equally significant function of not knowing must be represented. For an interpretation that seems quite correct to us might, upon the provision of further associations provided by the patient, prove to be incomplete or absolutely incorrect. So how do we bring the receptive capability of unknowing, which I argue maintains the analytic screen, into the interpretive situation?

It can be accomplished in my view only if the analyst takes himself as a subject in the analytical field. The analyst must reveal more of the analytical procedure to the analysand. However valuable his conclusions culled into the secondary process as an interpretive content, this is less meaningful, in my view, than the processes leading up to such an interpretation. When a patient needs to know why I have arrived at a comment, I will say how I have composed my interpretation. I do not always ask what associations come to the patient's mind, nor do I take up the question as a transference act. Sometimes a patient will not ask how I have arrived at an interpretation, but I will say that I want to indicate how I came by it, and I will trace my footsteps. This is one of the important features in both authorizing and limiting the function of the subjective.

I also differ with myself. When I am unhappy with a comment, either because I can tell from the patient's associations that I am wrong, or because further internal work supplants and alters a previous comment, I will criticize myself. And sometimes I will say, 'You know, that's absolutely wrong, isn't it?' or 'No, I'm wrong!' When I differ with myself, I destroy a previously established particle of knowledge. I then create its opposite, a space that now contains not knowing, but recognizes the presence of an unthought knowledge that may find its way to knowing. In the first sessions of an analysis, when I think that the patient is correcting a misperception on my part, or struggling too hard to adapt to an error on my part, I preface a correction with, 'You disagree'. **By endeavouring to introduce the factor of difference, we slowly establish the dialectics of difference**. I want to be free to differ with my analysand. I want him to be free to differ with me. And it is my experience that the analyst can establish the ability to differ early on in an analysis, even with patients who are seemingly so narcissistic or borderline that one would have thought they could not bear an interpretation that they found irritating or wrong. But I think they can. And I think it can be accomplished in a series of steps.

First, the analyst establishes a relation to his own subjectivity. He becomes a subject in the field of analysis and thinks about what he has said (his associations, as it were) in a manner that is similar to the way he considers the patient's associations.

Second, he recognizes each moment that the patient disagrees with him and very carefully articulates the patient's corrections. If the patient seems hesitant after I deliver an interpretation, I will say, 'But something about what I have said is not quite right'. If he mumbles in weak agreement, I will say 'I'm wrong' and analyse the patient's reluctance to correct me. And as we all know, more often than not, this will be accompanied by analysis of the analysand's discomfort over disagreeing.

Third, the analyst disagrees with the patient. To establish this as a non-traumatic and essential factor in analysis, the analyst should state it simply, in a relatively inconsequential moment, and as early as possible within the analysis: 'I find I have a different way of looking at what you have said, from your understanding of it'; 'You have said that the events you reported don't matter to you, but I disagree: they clearly do!'. Such interventions are common and essential examples of what I mean by disagreeing with the patient.

By establishing difference as an important part of the analytical sensibility, first by differing with myself, second by affirming the patient's disagreements with me, and finally by disagreeing with the patient's comments, I am more able to be openly confronting of an individual than might otherwise be the case. In recent work with a paranoid schizophrenic who would become enraged with me in sessions, I would often say, 'Well we disagree, don't we? You think X and you may be right. I happen to think Y', and this dialectic was very important because I was analysing his manic defences which was only possible because the analysand was by then accustomed to the dialectics of difference in our work.

Establishing a dialectics of difference with a patient, particularly with those who are very disturbed, is crucial to the successful management of the patient's regressive use of the analyst in the transference. An analyst who has established this as one of the rights of interrelating does not by any means disqualify himself as a subjective object or a self object. It simply means that he is a subjective object with a working 'not me' element that allows for the intersubjective processing of confict. I am pleased that amidst intense transference regression, when a patient needs to be very ill in my presence, I can both sustain this patient's need and maintain my function as an interpreting analyst. Disagreement with a patient, undramatically delivered yet processing appropriate affects, may be crucial to the working through of a transference psychosis.

The dialectic of difference is in part an unbinding process that checks the binding work of interpretation and lessens the likelihood that interpretation itself could become a resistance to the free associative process. When a patient can consistently anticipate what his analyst will say to him on the basis of reported free associations, then in all probability the analyst's interpretations have become a resistance to the analytic process.

Free association is somewhere between knowing and unknowing, binding and unbinding. As words are used to speak one's mind, it is possible to consider this a form of knowing and a binding procedure. But as one is meant to say whatever comes to mind regardless of how silly or senseless it seems, this invokes a different principle: of unknowing and of unbinding. Perhaps the inspired thought, the deep reflection, the de-repression of a memory, emerges from an optimal state of tension between the binding and unbinding process. Elsewhere (Bollas, 1987) I think of this as a tension between the conservative and the transformational processes, between the part of us that stores the experiences of life (in an unchanged state) and the part of us that transforms our experiences through symbolic representations.

The Analyst's Use of Free Association

When the psychoanalyst takes himself as an object of reflective consideration and analysis, he shares the patient's privileged position. This is not an indulgent and gratuitous sharing, but a discipline: a placing of one's self in a situation allowing for a rigorous analysis of the material. As this develops, the patient is, of course, in a position to reflectively consider and analyse the analyst's associations. This dialectic creates in the first place a field of signifiers that become lingual potential spaces for the evocation of repressed memories, or conserved self states, or for the arrival of new internal objects. But each accurate association adds to an increasing field of other accurate associations which taken together constitutes the construction of a processing medium, created from the psychical work of the analysis. If we think of Bion's theory of thinking – that it is the thought that creates the mental structure, and that structure derives from thinking – then the analyst's associations add to the mental structure being developed by the analysis.

I have little doubt that my use of the word 'association' as it comes from the analyst in the clinical hour will cause distress. What exactly do I mean? Am I suggesting that the analyst should say whatever comes to his mind without censorship? And if I am not saying this, then in what sense could his associations be truly 'free'?

As I think of it, the analyst's associations are musings. I muse on what a patient has said, or not said, or how the patient behaves. I say

'It occurs to me that ...' and proceed to say what I have in mind. I need further elaboration, and I need the patient's assistance. As I put my musings into language, I release signifiers into a potential chain of significations. The patient is free to discard associations that he thinks are on the wrong track, to select those with which he agrees, or those that speak to him, and to choose meanings from my musings. We could say that this is a process of free negation or free destruction, leading to free choice, and ultimately to free association. All patients need to destroy the analyst's associations in order to create out of such ideas a compatible set of views which feels about right to him. He develops a sense of trust in the process of thinking and uses this eventually to his own advantage.

We are well aware that in the practice of psychoanalysis these days we rarely see the neurotic patient who can freely associate, whose feelings are evident in the hour, whose resistances to speaking an uncomfortable thought are apparent, and whose dedication to understanding himself is a vital part of that therapeutic alliance that allows him to overcome resistances and work through unconscious conflict. What I am focusing on in this chapter is less relevant to work with the neurotic patient, than to the schizoid, borderline, and narcissistic patient – the individual who either cannot speak or who is so suspicious that he dare not; we need to place a different emphasis on the rules for the practice of psychoanalysis.

I think that the analyst needs to become a subject in the field of analysis, to make himself available for the patient in this way, and to establish a dialectics of difference: I think of this as part of an overall procedure of rendering psychic, of making psychic. By providing my associations to the patient's being or material, by musing on his presence, by remembering previous sessions, by posing certain questions, and seeking particular clarifications, I transform facts, or 'thing presentations', into psychic elements. Unreflected-upon elements such as the patient's mood, his manner, his statement of fact, even if it includes reporting a dream, are not psychic elements but something closer to what Bion (1962) means by beta factors: 'undigested facts'. The analytical process is a procedure for the making psychic which involves transforming facts into reflected objects, into mental objects, that in turn link up with other mental objects, to become part of intersecting chains of signification enriching a person's symbolic life, and also constructing a mental structure that can enhance the individual's mental processing of the facts of his existence.

Of course this view of the analyst's clinical orientation raises important matters of technique. How do we make our associations available to the analysand without it constituting an intrusion, or constituting a subtle takeover of the analysand's psychic life with the analyst's? Although I shall not take up these technical issues now, I will add that the analyst's reporting of his thoughts and associations must be momentary and set against the background of the patient's discourse and the silence that creates the analytic screen. A continuous, incessant flow of analyst's thoughts or observations would not be appropriate. The clinician must choose the right moment, select from and speak his associations in such a way as to create a set of mental objects that can be reflected upon by the analysand, in much the same way that both analyst and patient think of the dream. So, although there will be occasions when the analyst will elaborate associations, it is important for the analyst to stop in order to create a boundary around the association. In this way it is left as an object, to be considered by the patient, to be returned to after a period of hesitation, for potential usage. This principle of usage of oneself as a subject in the analytical field provides some overall guidance for the narrower technical issues.

Finally, it is my view that the process of rendering psychic, conceived of in the context of an object relationship that is characterized by a principle of dialectics of difference in which the analyst establishes himself as a subject in the field of analysis, constitutes a valid communication of what we can term the analytic sensibility. This sensibility is characterized by a paradox in our lives – that we are both subject and object. We provide the associations and then we reflect on them analytically. To be our own enigma is vital to our creativity. To be unknown to ourself is not necessarily a lack. We need unconsciousness in order to make a creative use of consciousness.

An analyst can establish himself as a subject without ever introducing into the analysis disclosures from his life or reflections on his own personality. To become a subject is not necessarily to talk about oneself to a patient, although in work with very disturbed adolescents or very psychotic patients it may be essential, in supporting their sense of belonging to the human race, to use examples from one's experience to say, 'Well, but that is human'. Otherwise, to be a subject refers to the analyst's psychical work on the patient's presence and narrative. Associating to a dream rather than interpreting it is a particularly valuable means of supporting the process of association. On hearing a patient's description of a fact in his life, I might say, 'That brings to my mind a dream you reported last month ...' I may say no more than this, identifying the dream, which leaves it up to the patient to associate, to utilize the psychic work, or to negate the analyst. Perhaps he will return to the analyst's associations later. If the patient refuses to be evoked by the analyst, or if he plays with the clinician's associations, either way the psychoanalyst has associated to facts, has transformed facts of life into psychical material, has linked past psychical material to the present, and has supported the rightful function of unconscious work.

While a dream serves as a particularly unique potential space for the evocation, establishment, and working through of the patient's internal world, I also take a patient's description of events and render them psychic if they bring other reported events to my mind. I also comment on the patient's presence and manner of being in a session. 'You seem perplexed', 'You seem tired', You look happy!' are remarks I make to sponsor reflection. But with a particularly difficult patient, who might demand my accounting for this comment, I may become the primary subject in the session as I associate to my impressions. The patient may seek to analyse me, perhaps in a triumphantly paranoid way, and if so, I will listen carefully to his angry comments and agree with him where appropriate, thus validating his estranged right to disagree, to have his own views. Some patients need to explore the analyst's way of knowing before they can commit themselves to a self discovery, so my 'analysis' or 'our analyses' of how I may come to feel the way I do, or think what I do, can fulfil an essential need in such a person to be seen and reflected by a good and sane container.

The object that is the source of the analyst's reflections, that establishes a limited but distinct view of the analyst as subject, is the patient. The analyst redirects himself to reporting associations, memories from and about the analysis, and senses of something – all within the context of the patient's presence.

The Rights of Idiom

P erhaps it is clear that I am linking the countertransference and the use of the self-analytic element in the establishment of the analyst as a subject with the concept of a dialectics of difference. I argue that this constitutes a particular relation to subjectivity, in which the analyst uses the fact of subjective idiom to his and his patient's psychoanalytic advantage. It is a way of acknowledging that personal idiom always mediates the unconscious and its laws. Psychoanalysts make interpretations, they invent meaning; they do not discover the meaning conveyed by the patient. No two analysts would ever say the same thing to the same patient.

By establishing difference (with himself as well as the patient) as a crucial factor in the analytic work, the analyst enables himself to introduce a differentiated intellectual affectivity in the sessions. This is crucial to our comments to patients, our long struggles, and to our celebration of the analysand when our 'Of course!' emphasizes some aspect of the life instincts.

Sometimes we have no choice but to be bewildering. A person whom I have termed a normotic (Bollas, 1987) – an individual who is abnormally normal and who aims to de-subjectify the self in order to become a thing-object – needs to experience the pleasures of entertaining the subjective which I think has to come from the analyst. I am sure we can all think of cases where the analyst comes up against a patient who for one reason or other is bereft of signs of life, and the analyst's speech and affect are the life of the hour. Being strange to such a person, through one's comments, evokes his interest and brings to the analytic situation a certain imaginative freedom.

Some patients need me to establish the right of idiom, which I represent, not only through the content of my remarks but through my relation to subjectivity itself. One might object to this principle, not only on the grounds that it seems to violate analytic neutrality, but because it appears to place some mystical value on the irrational, giving the analyst an omnipotence that would be an abuse of the patient's transference. Is this not a call for whimsy, fancy, mysticism, isolated subjectivism; a call for any instinct to find its gratification through analytic acting out?

I believe all the above is possible. Were an analyst to establish as an ongoing act only the statements from association, or to indulge himself in the private pleasure of an odd remark, conveyed simply to put the patient in a difficult position, then, of course, this is abusive. Of course, so called 'ordinary analytic interpretation' is capable of the same valence, and perhaps it is even more disturbing because it might be delivered by an analyst as the truth, to be accepted by the patient, or worked through, where 'worked' could be read as in a psychic assault. The analyst who chooses to establish himself incrementally as a subject in his clinical work must, of course, come by the discipline needed to introduce this factor without it usurping the analysand's psychic uses of the analytic process and the transference object. Thus a sense of judgement and tact is essential here, as it is in any other analytic practice. I find that I am more mentally concentrated and thoughtful when representing the subjective (of content or personal idiom) than when I work in more classical ways. I believe my commitment to my own discipline, to my own manner of practice, is conveyed to the patient, and, as long as I carefully analyse the patient's response to my 'presence', and correct myself when I am wrong, I think the chance of error on the side of increasing analytic omnipotence or acting out is minimized.

The analyst must decide the appropriateness of providing his associations to the analysand's material. It should never usurp the patient's free association, even if the patient seems 'stuck' or is silent for long periods of time. Indeed, it should serve to facilitate the free movement of ideas, feelings, recollections, and self states in the analysand. In a way the analyst's associations may be the missing link in the patient's chain of associations, which is consistent with one view of projective identification: that the analyst carries split off ideas projected into him by the patient. I do not know if this is true of all associations carried by an analyst while with the analysand. Ordinarily I do not think the analyst should declare an association as patient-inspired; instead he should be an imaginative partner to the analysand, who will appreciate the analyst's effort of intelligence as the work of an independent mind involved in that complex interrelating that is psychoanalysis.

By establishing a working dialectic with the patient, one which cultivates rhetorical positions that affirm the difference between any two human subjectivities, the analyst sustains the intermediate nature of interpretation, as it can only be a comment 'placed' between patient and analysand. The analyst's interpretation of the patient's discourse, being, or relating is always hazardous, as is any effort undertaken by one person to claim knowledge about the mental contents of any other person. But this peril is no different from our 'collection' of interpretations, as its ultimate source must never be certain to us. To some this is a less than satisfactory account of the discipline of analytic interpretation, which, it is argued, is capable of exactitude. For me, however, any interpretation is always only partly true, as the narrowing of focus essential to the organization of comment about another person inevitably means that all other possible comments are at that moment unspoken. And the interpretation of that moment will be altered, perhaps completely abandoned, with the provision of further material during the course of analytic time.

By associating to an analysand's comments I aim to reveal more of the nature of those processes within myself that eventually go into the making of an interpretation. I intend the patient to participate in the evolution of my own thinking on the way to knowing. And vital to this endeavour, it seems to me, is the establishment of the right to disagree, so that neither analysand nor analyst is foreclosed by a policy of adaptation.

I do not know the sources of interpretation. I do not know why one day with patient A I find myself concentrating on A's word presentations, whilst the next day I might be mulling over his creation within me of some object in his past. Nor do I understand why one day with A I wander off, barely listening to what he is saying, yet on another day find myself acutely attentive to his silence. Some analysts might argue that each of my states of mind (and hence the origins of interpretation) is the work of a patient's projective identification. But this stretches a meaningful concept to an absurd extreme, to the point of turning the patient–analyst relation into a kind of seance, where the analyst is a spiritualist who lives out the lives of others: dead or alive. I am certain that each of my experiences with an analysand is determined in part by their particular idiom, but I am equally convinced that my own unconscious processes are active in the genre of interpretive choice: whether I comment on words, object relations, moods, or the patient's self-experiencing.

I believe that all patients do sense the particular way his or her analyst organizes 'the material'. They also correctly perceive aspects of the analyst's personality. By establishing himself as a subject in the analysis, I think the psychoanalyst simply gives a more honest and analytically fruitful place to the subjective origins of personality, unconscious organization, and analytic practice. A patient might wish me to be an all knowing idealized figure, and certain transference needs are so intense that this is how I am constructed, but by being different, by establishing more openly how I think what I do, a patient is free to *think me* as an object. As I correct myself, as the patient corrects me, as I challenge the patient, as he challenges me, I have found what to me is a more trustworthy analytic mutuality in sessions. I believe that what I describe is a form of play in the analytic situation. Clearly I work this way because I am more comfortable with it and because I believe ·in it. I disagree both with those analysts who systematically and rigorously translate the patient's discourse into transference interpretations (all in the name of pure analysis) and with those who believe that each patient needs constant affective and interpretive adjustment from the analyst in order to feel understood. The first practice erodes the analysand's self-analytic capability and distorts the unconsciousness of the unconscious, leading to a secondary process over mentalization of psychic life, as virtually any discourse can be immediately translated into a transference response. The second practice expels the analytic element from the scenes of the analytic situation, as the clinician seeks positions of identification with the analysand to provide an empathically attuned response.

But each of these perspectives – the analyst as subject, as translator of discourse into transference, as empathizer, or as a minimalist auditor of the murmurings of the other – is important if understood as one element in the total field of analytic practice. We should find a way to integrate the many elements of these differing emphases in order to create our own practice. There is no such thing as *the* practice of psychoanalysis. For better and for worse, there is only each analyst's attempts, a fact of our daily lives that hopefully keeps us interested in whatever any other analyst currently favours as a new dimension in theory and practice, whilst inevitably sustaining in us a reticence to convert our analytic ideology into the analysand's fate.

4

The Psychoanalyst's Celebration
of the Analysand

I if one of the aims of a psychoanalysis is to analyse as much as is humanly possible of what the analysand presents, and if we are not to be deterred by conventional social niceties in the pursuit of speaking the truth, then no particular feature of a person should be subject to an exclusion clause.

This ethic has often been a rallying cry to analysts who take it as an almost specially appointed task to analyse the patient's destructive mental processes. One of the facets of this emphasis is the technical difficulty of causing distress to a patient's narcissistic self valuation by focusing on disavowed destructiveness. I believe that this emphasis in psychoanalysis is indeed quite valuable, but I am puzzled by the fact that in the psychoanalytic literature, the rigorous analysis of destructive processes and the negative transference are presented as if this were a particularly onerous task. My experience is that most analysands are consciously troubled by their destructive thoughts, feelings, and actions, and though they do, of course, resist analysis of such factors of the personality in the here and now transference, they nonetheless issue the analyst with an implied licence to pursue his course of analysing the complex mental processing of hate. My puzzlement turns to something else – I suppose to this writing of it – as I try to grapple with what I consider to be a worrying exclusion, at least in the literature of psychoanalysis, of a more analytically difficult task – the psychoanalysis of the patient's life instincts: his love of the analyst, his creative integrations in analytic work, his admirable accomplishments in life (and analysis).

I find that some analysts are often too willing to head for analysis of the negative transference, ostensibly because this is where the rough work is, but in fact because they often feel on surer ground if they are analysing hate. Do we need to oppose the patient? If not, then perhaps in clinical presentations we need to advertise to our colleagues just how clever we are, and this often means demonstrating how we deconstructed the manifest text of the patient's material, or un-flinchingly analysed the patient's unconscious negative transference. When we are in such a mood – and I suppose some analysts may practise within this mood their entire career – a patient's affection for the analyst, inspiring a particularly glowing account of the analyst, will only be interpreted as a defensive idealization of the analyst: and the split-off hate is pursued. I expect such a view is partly correct. Hate must be somewhere. But in analysing idealization this way I think affection and love are discarded not because hate is more important to spot, but because some analysts are not as comfortable articulating the positive (the life instinct) as they are confronting the dark forces of the death instinct.

This is a preamble to my particular intent which is to address what I term **the analyst's celebration of the analysand**. If the psychoanalyst's intelligent marking of an analysand's negative transference involves him in a slight temperamental intensity, a concentrated thoughtful-ness, the psychoanalyst's celebration of the analysand involves him in an equally slight, though noticeable, temperamental mood toward a celebration of the patient – an affective registration on the analyst's part of the presence of a life instinct factor in the patient. I do not mean the analyst's dispensing of approval as such, although I do mean the analyst's use of his understanding of mental life to recognize the positive factors in a patient in the same way that he brings analytic understanding to bear when confronting the patient's negative processes. In the same way that analysis of the death instincts should not be condemnation, so too analysis of the life instincts should not be primarily the analyst gratifying the patient with praise. Confrontation of the death and life instincts must be an act of psychoanalytic intelligence, so that the patient learns something about himself that he may put to use in his own way.

Nonetheless, as I think that the analyst's acts of intelligence differ in temperament when analysing these two factors (life and death), I must make it clear what I mean by the celebration of the analysand. At this point I shall provide clinical examples and return to a more complete discussion of the issues when I have satisfied myself that I have adequately demonstrated what I mean.

Elena

E lena's psychotherapist presented her in a case workshop. She is eleven, and an only child of parents who are exacting and obsessional personalities. Their house is spotlessly clean, as if no person has ever lived in it, and in family consultations they try to take control of the sessions, in particular to prevent any conflicts between themselves from being revealed. They have no problems.

Elena had come to treatment because of night terrors and sudden withdrawn behaviour at school. Her distress had, at least, an apparently specific onset. One day when she was watching television, something she did quite often, she saw a particularly disturbing programme. It was a monster film and suddenly the monster's face disintegrated. Elena was shocked and disoriented by this. She refused to go to sleep, and eventually her parents took her to hospital.

The therapist found Elena to be a very sweet and likeable little girl who was, however, the carbon copy of her parents. She was distressingly tidy, in dread of making any mess, critical of herself and of her analyst.

One day she made a drawing of a large institution. It had many floors and resembled the hospital and, in some respects, her home. In the basement of the building she drew a television. In one of the upper rooms she created a spider and said, 'I will make a *big* spider!' The therapist replied, 'You have created something fearful, like black spiders with their cobweb'. Elena replied cuttingly, 'Really I wanted to make a big bicycle, but I can't manage'.

It's not difficult to see what the therapist meant by this comment. She knew that the child had suffered a serious outbreak of symptomatology after the television episode, and as she noted that the child first drew the television and then created the spider, she assumed this to be a free associative elaboration of the original fear. And I'm sure that in some respects she was correct, but I disagreed with her intervention.

The therapist had reported to the workshop that Elena's mother had a sudden, almost violent temper. She was a very demanding person, exceptionally determined to have order, and whenever Elena made a mess or engaged in ordinary childhood mucking about, the mother would fly into a rage. Therefore, when I heard about Elena's response to the television monster's disintegrating face, I thought that this must be, in some respects, a 'screen' for Elena's emotional experience of the mother's face that disintegrates with rage into monstrousness. And if we link Elena's enraged response to the mother's abuse of her, then this disintegrating monster becomes even more fearful as it bears the vindictive features of Elena's destructive feeling.

To sleep is to dream. To have a dream one creates the dream space, much as one enters the cinema to see a film. The dream space contains the dream content. If the dream screen bursts into being a monster under the assaults of projection, then the dream attacks the dreamer. This nightmare may indeed be too much to bear.

Elena lived in a near psychotic fear of her own inner life, in particular, her instinctual life. I inferred from the material that her mother had attacked her instinctual life and subliminatory processes, and that Elena had never experienced a container to receive the instincts. When Elena 'makes' a spider, with the television (the looking monster mummy) safe in the basement, she introduces the representation of instinctual life. Indeed she seems pleased with this by stressing she is making the spider (rather than saying in a more schizoid way, 'Here is a spider') and that it will be a big spider. This is a big moment.

I suggested that it would have been a better intervention if the therapist had first celebrated the arrival of instinctual life. This could have been accomplished through a simple comment such as, 'Ah! A spider!' to give an affective recognition of the value of instinct representation. Of course, this assumes that I am correct about the spider representing instincts. I take it to be a little creature who, though mirroring the mother's obsessionality (it spins webs), exemplifies the animate, the silent movement of urges, and I am reminded of the common psychoanalytic understanding of the spider as a representation of the female genitals. However, if I were wrong, if the spider represented a fragment of a watching superego, then the child would correct me and the 'Ah, a spider!' could change to 'So, not such a nice thing, after all!' In any event, the aim of a comment here is to give an affective response to the child's representations. This affective response is part of what I mean by celebrating the analysand, as it supports the evolution of the patient's 'imaginative elaboration of bodily functions' (Winnicott, 1988, p. 51).

I think Elena's response to the therapist's interpretation lends credence to my view that the spider represents instinctual life as she says that after all it was not to be a spider but a big bicycle. In other words, because she feels the therapist has failed to enjoy her representation of instinct, Elena withdraws instinct representation and picks an ego object: a bicycle which is man-made and represents the movements of the body ego rather than the perambulations of the instinctual soma.

In another moment in the session Elena draws a beautiful girl on a horse and, as the therapist remains silent, erases the girl and puts an erect boy on the horse, leaving the girl as only a faint outline. Of course this is wonderfully suggestive and useful material for analysis, but I think Elena wanted the therapist to admire the girl on the horse, to say something like, 'Ah, a beautiful girl!' and failing that, she erases the girl and substitutes a boy.

Of course I do think that after celebrating the arrival of the girl's sexuality, it is important to analyse its meaning. But meaning must follow on from establishment, just as successful representation is a priority over the analysis of the representation. Another way of considering this, in terms of Bion's concept of container and contained, is to state that celebration of the analysand's representations announces the analyst's generative container function. This receptivity to representation, an attitude akin to a kind of *pleasure*, plays an important role in eliciting further representations from the patient.

The psychoanalytic facilitation of the arrival of mental representations of the true self is an important and inadequately discussed part of the analytic technique. When we say, 'Ah! A spider!' to an Elena, we encourage the representational process, not the specific content of the representation. This is not a moment when the analyst suggests to the patient that he likes spiders and is pleased that the child has drawn something that he likes. It is an occasion when the analyst celebrates the articulation of the true self. The spider is the child's creation. What the analyst supports, then, is the child's creativity, and he in turn notifies the child that he can mentally contain, process, and facilitate the child's elaboration of true self articulations. As such the child experiences the analyst's celebration of his representations as ego enhancing, because the analyst conveys to the patient that he has the internal space there to entertain the child's further elaborations. Premature interpreting of the content of the child's communications may be experienced as a refusal of true self elaboration. The patient might experience the analyst's translations into the analyst's frame of mind as an act of intellectual appropriation. This may not foreclose analytic interpretation, the child may still produce associations, but such productions would not be articulative elaborations of the true self. The patient's mind, as a now somewhat split-off part of the psyche, would be producing material for the psychoanalyst's mind. This is the work of the false self, now producing for the other, rather than expressing the true self which goes into hiding.

The psychoanalyst's affective celebration of the arrival of instinctual representations and the articulated elaborations of the true self is a prerequisite to any subsequent interpretation of content. Indeed, I think simple representation of true self, as a means of freeing up true self, can be therapeutic in its own right. I am reminded of the remarkable work of Mary Walker of the Mardan Center in Costa Mesa, California. Mrs Walker is a former principal of an ordinary school and some thirty years ago joined the staff of an alternative school for the education of severely disturbed, acting out children. A recent addition to their student body, for example, had taken his mother hostage with a gun pointed to her head. The area police were called, the house sealed off from the outside world, and its modest stucco frame illuminated by the lights from the police helicopter hovering above. After twelve hours of siege the boy surrendered his loaded gun to the police, and some six months later, at the Mardan Center, he was doing well in school for the first time. So this school takes very distressed children and helps them. And each of the grade school children has one hour a week with Mrs Walker who sits in her sunny, toy-filled room, and presides over a sandpit. Apart from the occasional encouraging word she says nothing. She simply watches as the children create imaginary scenes in the sand (many villages, army scenes, and so on). And over the years she has been the object of very moving visits to the school by former students who wish to see her again and thank her for what she did. Such visits are by no means uncommon; indeed, I have been present when four people have been to see her, and on each occasion the now adult person embraces her or simply stands and stares at her and thanks her for allowing them to be alone in the presence of a figure who does not interfere with their creations.

Like Winnicott's theory of hesitation, which follows on from his presentation of a spatula to infants (see p. 198), Walker's *absolute neutral space* permits the distressed child to enjoy the rights of representation. Although this model should not be taken as an alternative to psychoanalytic interpretation, there is much the analyst can learn from Mary Walker. The true self must be true to be itself. The child and adult analysand must feel an originating inner reality behind their representations. For this to occur, there must be a time lapse. The analyst's comments should ordinarily follow as reflections on the true self, not as translations of them into the analyst's frame of mind.

In *The Shadow of the Object* (Bollas, 1987, pp. 221–5) I wrote about a patient who was manic depressive. And one feature of my work with him, my intense confrontations of his delusions, was contingent upon my celebration of his capabilities. I do not think that George would ever have been able to bear my confrontative analysis of him had I not also always enjoyed his creativity. For example, in the midst of somewhat long and occasionally tiresome and irritating lectures George would state something quite brilliantly. When this occurred, I would interrupt him to say, 'Well, what you say is quite extraordinary', or 'I *do* admire your beautiful analogy'. I stated these thoughts because they were true. He was brilliant and at times capable of moving articulations of complex ideas.

I am reminded of my work with the late Paula Heimann, who supervised my first psychoanalytic case. I was treating a poly-symptomatic hysteric who was a furiously intelligent woman whose hysterical skill was way beyond my clinical acumen. Try as I did to interpret to her in the transference, I nearly always worded myself clumsily and my errors simply released more of my patient's furies. She would tear each of my comments to shreds, except when I stuck to simple clarifications which she allowed me. Paula Heimann quite admired and enjoyed my analysand's pluck, and what was at first only misery for me – I think I established an altogether new low in my narcissistic injury spectrum – moved eventually (very slowly, I'm afraid) to increased competence on my part. This was achieved because I took to heart Paula Heimann's insistence that when my patient boxed me in (which she did all the time), I should congratulate her: 'Ah! So you have trounced me once again!' I remember the first time I said it to the patient. Almost in a vocalization continuous with what I said she replied, 'Yes, I did!' And then there was a silence. The first *good* silence in the analysis. And I think it was partly created by the analysand's success in getting me to stop trying so hard to analyse her. She was quite rightly furious with my effort to translate her discourse into my own terms.

When Jerome (see chapter 2) mocked me in a session, I laughed, and such laughter is another interpretive comment that celebrates the analysand. I then said 'Well, I *do* laugh, because, frankly, it is hilarious'. And it was terribly funny. It is painful for me to have to say that some analysts would regard such mocking of me as only a sign of a negative transference, the analysand aiming to diminish me and empty me of my mind. Envy of me would be the motivating factor. But Jerome's mocking was a form of familiarization, a subjectification of me. In that moment I became his subjective object and he was saying: 'You see, object, I have my version of you, don't I!' an accomplishment that was an important development in his analysis.

Another patient who was schizoid and unaccustomed to object relationships, although he was skilled in alternative internal object construction, apologized profusely whenever an internal object representation of me 'spilled out' of him. When he would criticize me, often quite legitimately, for an incorrect interpretation, he would say how sorry he was, and often I would say, 'But why shouldn't you correct me? Why shouldn't you have a go at me?' The patient found these comments strikingly unbelievable. He sincerely thought that I would find his attacks on me so maddening that I would take some dreadful revenge on him. And along with my celebration of his aggressive uses of me, it was essential to analyse why he feared such use of me.

'Ah! So I am an idiot!' I may say to a patient who is tentatively and anxiously trying to convey angry feelings. If the patient retracts the comment and tries to make me feel better, assuming at that moment that I am damaged, I might say, 'If you feel I'm a dummy, why shouldn't you say so?' implicitly celebrating their right to attack.

Or I may say, 'So! You are enjoying having a go at me, yes?' and by putting it this way to a patient, I celebrate the nature of their cathexis of me as an object in an object relationship. It is important, of course, to differentiate between aggression that is akin to a libidinal use of the object, a form of play with the object, and a violent destruction, the aim of which is to denigrate the analyst and maintain omnipotent control over what's left of him.

Because of the evolution of the false self, or excessive anxiety leading to depressive withdrawal, some patients have no belief in their right to exist. They may be masters at constructing inner objects but surprisingly inexperienced at object relationships. Analysis of the mental processes of internal object relations must be complemented by facilitation of object relating, and for that to occur the analysand must feel that the analyst values (celebrates) the movement from inner object relations to object relating. In order for this to occur, the analyst will have to announce, 'I am an object ready for your usage', which is part of object relationships.

The analyst who celebrates the arrival of instinctual and true self representations provides an important linking function between the exclusively inner world and the actual world. In this intermediate position the analyst uses a certain affective responsiveness to receptively contain and process aspects of the patient's emotional reality which the patient feels compelled to keep to himself. Needless to say, this involves the analyst in a function somewhat different from the classical model of the neutral voice of the analyst; certainly the analyst's voice bears feelings in the above (see pp. 176–7). But I do not think such feelings are affective discharges or extraneous migrations of the analyst's personality into the sessions. I think this use of feeling is a provision of affective association to the patient's material. It is like an analytic clarification which helps the flow of free associations, or ideas, but in this case it is more facilitative of the flow of feelings, self states, and object relations.

The psychoanalyst celebrates the true self through his affective response to its presence! All of the interventions described above are affective statements; they establish an experiential domain for true self expression and experience of the object world, because such comments indicate to the patient that the analyst–object is emotionally responsive to the patient's state of being. 'So I'm an idiot!' or 'Why shouldn't you correct me?' are not only statements, they are affective *links* to the patient's true self, which *moves*, through the use of the object, so the spirit of the analyst's comments links up with the patient's affect to establish *movement*. These comments become introjected by the patient, not for the intellectual merits of their content – they are very simple ideas – but because they are valuable mental objects for true self usage. When the analyst speaks in such a way, it is as if he says 'True self? This way! Through here!' The patient's idiom is then able to use the analyst's analytic personality as a complex field of mental objects through which to elaborate itself, an articulation that is part of the need to develop this true self, which is a feature of the destiny drive. In the analysis the patient cannot know mentally what the course of true self is. It is, as I have suggested, not a script which is to be acted out, but a complex set of assumptions, attitudes, and inner laws which come alive only through lived experience. True self is this experiencing in the moment. It is the movement of the person in life, a progression if it expresses this inner core and if the objects through which the person moves are facilitative ones.

Because I value the function of intense analytic confrontation of an analysand, when the patient recreates disturbed family relations and the emotional turbulence derived from pathological family relations, I think it is incumbent on me to pay careful attention to the analysand's ego abilities and to support, by celebration and then interpretation, those capabilities. And as I use my feelings in my interpretive work, when confronting an analysand, I also use feelings when celebrating that person.

If my examples have been clear, then I hope that there is minimal confusion over whether by celebration I mean gratification. Nonetheless, I can expect an objection to my views on the grounds that I am undermining the analytic–interpretive process with a subtle system of reward and deprivation. I do not think this is an unfair objection, as I have noted, when presenting these views, that often celebration is taken to mean the analyst stating, 'I approve of you'. So this is a problem.

To my mind this issue of whether I am celebrating representation and object relating or gratifying the patient's wish to please me is likely to be one of the early problems that arises in the clinical application of these ideas. Perhaps some clinicians will take this as an occasion to cue the patient towards the presentation of the positive. But this is only one of the ordinary yet difficult tasks clinicians face in developing a technique suited to the facilitation of life instinct representations and object relating. (Similar problems beset those analysts who urge colleagues to analyse the negative transference. The technical difficulty in such a work is how to direct the patient's attention to his destructive mental actions without the analyst becoming a harsh split off superego, thereby stealing from the patient the very psychic structure that is essential to modifying destructive thoughts.) The problem we face in celebrating the analysand is in not allowing this to be a form of stimulation, gratification, or false self adaptation.

In either case, however, the analyst has available his assessment of the analysand's response to his interpretations and his ability to comment on the patient's response. So if it is clear that a patient feels that I am rewarding him for a factor in his personality and seeking more of my comments, then this should be interpreted to the patient: 'I can see that my comment on your abilities has stimulated a wish to have more such remarks from me'. But I have found problems with this kind of intervention to be of an altogether different and rather surprising kind.

Many analysands mistrust the analyst when he comments on a constructive side of their personality. This is often the result of its sheer strangeness. Some individuals are simply unaccustomed to having a positive appraisal of any aspect of themselves. This may be because, sadly, they have rarely received any such recognition from a parent. But it may also be because they lack any part of their own mind which celebrates the positive parts of their personality. By celebrating an aspect of the analysand, the analyst may introduce a factor which is relatively unknown to the patient. Sometimes, when this is the case, the patient will act as if he has not heard the analyst and proceed to talk about something else without acknowledging the analyst's intervention.

When this is true, the analyst needs to follow up a celebration with an analysis of the patient's response, including their real confusion over how to receive such a comment. The patient may feel that the analyst has injected libido into a dehydrated but familiar form of object relating (of the schizoid type) and sincerely may not know how to process this factor which seems to be entirely external to them.

On other occasions the patient may experience the analyst's comment as unbelievable because it seems to fulfil an intense though secret wish on the analysand's part. Such patients believe something really odd has happened; the analyst has commented on some aspect of them as if fulfilling powerful wishes. If this is the case, then it is possible for the analyst to comment on how upsetting this intervention is because it seems to realize strong wishes in the sessions. Perhaps this will lead to an analysis of the underlying fantasies of what will happen to the patient if he represents his wishes.

Perhaps the patient's wishes are so enmeshed with the object that the analysand understands such interventions as only valuable because the analyst seems to approve. The approval of the object, therefore, can be seen to have usurped the intrinsic value of the true self, and if so, then this may necessitate analysis of the false self. When this is the situation, it is a deeply moving experience for a patient to understand that celebration of their abilities is valued because it is one of the human rights that we have and not because it is what is demanded or expected of us.

Another common reaction is for a patient to feel a sudden despair. They interpret the analyst's comments on their abilities as an indication that the analyst is no longer going to take their problems as they perceive them seriously. Ego abilities and generative object relations are regarded as less valuable, less near the core of man, than painful issues and intense conflict. When the patient feels this way, he may panic because he thinks the analyst has given up on him by trying to fob him off with what he experiences as compliments.

The above reactions, which are more common than states of relief brought on by celebration, indicate, in my view, just how very difficult it is for the analyst to work in this area. I find that a patient's response to a positive comment is far more complex and conflicting than the response to what they experience as a painful confrontation. It is not easy to provide a celebration of the analysand. I find that it necessitates a very particular kind of concentration and work in me in order to 'deliver' the comment, to attend to the immediate response, and to follow this up with any analysis that is necessary.

Indeed, the analytic effort to celebrate the analysand's ego abilities (the ego that is essential to processing the true self) often results in a prolonged and difficult struggle with the analysand, who will endeavour to conceal his feelings and abilities in order to defeat the analyst's effort to facilitate his personal evolution. I find this struggle more difficult than dealing with the analysand who wishes to sustain a pure image of himself at the cost of splitting off the destructive parts of himself. If you challenge the patient's destruction, the analytic evidence of it is fortunately bountiful, particularly in the negative transference. It is easy to feel supported by the evidence. When aiming to celebrate elements of the patient, however, the analyst may be without much evidence (other than his own conviction or intuition), particularly when the patient becomes totally dismissive of this analytic endeavour.

Indeed a patient may have achieved an irreversible destruction of his life instincts. He may have become grimly determined to punish the true self by not celebrating ego abilities and therefore evolving the true self. Giovanni, a patient I saw for some two years of analysis, did defeat my efforts to occasionally celebrate him. He was a talented person who had suffered persistent mental cruelty from his father in the oedipal and latency periods. As a result of this he was deeply, and I fear unremittingly, identified with the father's crushing of the true self. He insisted that I regard him as a 'worthless piece of shit' as he was fond of saying. Following my comments, he would lift his hands in the air as if praying to a god, and say, 'Ah, Bollas! You are such a good man. What you say makes sense of course, but it is wasted, ABSOLUTELY wasted on a piece of shit like me.' He would then move to a kind of hissing and sighing laugh. I was unable to reach him, even when he lost his job (and I reduced his fee for one year of analysis). He moved out of the country to be with his girlfriend, and I don't know what has become of him.

One of the most difficult issues to discuss in the course of an analysis is the pleasure the analysand takes in being analysed and that mutual pleasure that may constitute a very important feature of the analytic couple. If one aim of analysis is to comment on all the features of the patient's experience of the analyst, how do we discuss mutual pleasure? What do I mean by mutual pleasure?

I am not talking about mutual erotic excitement, of the excitement from the id, but of something that at times is in the nature of ego excitement that is mutual and at other times simply gratification at the effectiveness of working together. At one point in the course of his analysis, Jerome (see pp. 50–8) had developed a very different new self, free of paranoid complexities, and able to speak himself, and use me as an analyst in a very creative manner. It became clear, however, that he needed me to find some way to talk about his affection for me, an affection that was an outcome of our collaboration together, not a transference expression of love of mother or father. His feelings emerged out of the pleasures of being analysed and were sustained by his forthright presentation of material that was painful but needed analysing. In the middle of one session, after working on a dream together which produced a very fruitful interpretation, he was really almost ecstatic. I decided to comment on the pleasures of our relationship. I said, 'Not a bad team, are we!' and he replied instantly, 'No, not half bad at all. In fact, terrific.' There was a silence and I said, 'I have been very tough on you. No doubt I will be again, as you have been on me, which is as it should be. So it's as well for us to comment on our pleasure at being and working together.' He agreed and talked fully about his gratitude to me, his love, if I can put it that way, of contributing to his analysis and of my valuation of his contributions, and his pleasure in attending the sessions.

It is useful to be reminded of a non-psychoanalytic source to define the word 'pleasure'. Webster's: 'The gratification of the senses or of the mind: agreeable sensations or emotions: the excitement, relish, or happiness produced by enjoyment or the expectation of good ... opposed to pain.' Given the sober reputation of Mr Webster, let us see if we can consider the nature of pleasure within the analytic situation.

Pleasure is a 'gratification of the senses or of the mind'. Well right away we have trouble as we are very familiar indeed with the refrain that the analyst must not gratify the patient. But does this also mean that the patient and the analyst should not find gratification in the analytic process? I am sure this cannot be. Certainly we would agree that analysis does indeed gratify the mind. Free association is gratifying in this sense, as is the giving and receiving of a good interpretation. Being understood is gratifying. What of the gratification of the senses? Well I am sure that lying on the couch is sensationally gratifying. As is hearing the analyst's voice, or upon leaving the session having a look at him. Talking to the analyst is in itself a sensational experience, as talking to the analyst is different from talking to anyone else. Words seem to count for more.

Pleasure is an 'agreeable sensation or emotion', and we know that of course many sensations in analysis are agreeable, and each patient has pleasing emotional experiences. The positive transference, for example, is a pleasing emotion.

Webster also speaks of 'excitement', 'relish', and 'happiness produced by enjoyment or expectation of good', which is a frank and useful way to describe the analysand's response to and expectation of certain interpretations. It is undeniable that analysands take pleasure in a correct interpretation, even though that is not our prime intent in delivering a comment, nor indeed, even the patient's primary intent in being an analysand. However, pleasure does emerge, and as it emerges in the course of the analysis, it is important for the analyst at least to talk about it and to indicate to the patient and himself the pleasure of being an analytic couple working together in fruitful ways.

When an analyst celebrates the analysand I think we refer to the clinician's emphasis on the patient's ego processes and object usages in the therapeutic situation. I am not referring to the analyst's praise of a patient's accomplishments outside the analytical situation, but rather to the analysand's generative use of the analysis. The good enough use of the analyst is pleasurable. In a certain sense it is an operational manifestation of the life instincts. The patient takes pleasure in the analyst's skill and in turn uses the analytical object to good effect. When the analyst celebrates the patient's ego processes and object usage, he facilitates the analysand's true self progression.

I hope in this brief exposition that I have illuminated how I think the analyst should celebrate his analysand. I think this is a crucial part of good analytic technique in which the analyst facilitates the patient's object relating by celebrating representation of instinct, ego, and object relational pleasures. This constitutes a different use of the analyst than the more strictly defined classical technique, but is an essential pathway to the analytical understanding of the patient's object relating.

5

The Psychoanalyst's
Multiple Function

Psychoanalytic interpretation produces what Bion (1962) terms 'psychoanalytic objects' – formulations generated by the psychoanalyst that give birth to ideas that may be of use to the patient and analyst. By conventional standards psychoanalysts say quite strange things to analysands, and analysands are rather tolerant of the analysts' psychoanalytic nature. Most patients know that what enters the analyst's mind and exits as his discourse is peculiar to the analytic situation and that interpretations are socially odd creative objects.

The psychoanalyst's creativity is essential to the patient's use of the analytic process. When the clinician puts a new idea to a patient, this mental object may open inner spaces for experiencing and knowing. The analytic object is in this sense being used and then discarded as the patient moves through the comment to another idea.

Although it is difficult for an analysand to describe an analysis, a patient who has had a good analysis will know the major problems besetting his personality and understand how these problems have been worked through. He will also have a sense that his true self has been released into further establishment and articulation. It may be difficult for him to explain how he feels personally more real and creative, but he may be able to link up increased personality freedom with his analyst's technique. He may recall that the analyst's interpretations seemed to 'open up' new doors of perception, a memory of what I would describe as the analyst's provision of analytic objects.

The analyst's discovery of psychoanalytic ideas constitutes his provision of objects that can be used by the patient to evoke repressed memories, to collect split thoughts, or to facilitate new self states. It is *the patient's use of* such objects that determines whether an idea becomes an insight. Analytic insight is always a potential, but its successful accomplishment is a rarity. The analyst's interpretive work is not insightful: it can only generate insight in the other.

This may be a less controversial point than I think; perhaps all analysts would agree. But I am concerned that some psychoanalysts, who place a particularly high value on the unwavering interpretation of the here and now transference, seem to believe that by a constant translation of a patient's discourse *into* transference interpretations, the patient will move from a primitive level of functioning to a less fractured state of mind, less troubled by anxiety of a persecutory kind and ennobled by a kind of curative depression.

The question arises: is this analytic work insightful? Has the patient enhanced his understanding of himself and developed a capacity for insight? The answer is yes and no.

Hesitation and Insight

I have no doubt that the analysands of analysts who favour a highly interpretive translation of patient discourse and behaviour into the transference paradigm discover a great deal about mental processes. Further, they can link moods and affects to mental processes that have been unconscious. Such a technique is a useful feature in an analysis, and there are indeed periods of time when I work in an intensely interpretive manner. I tend not do this at the beginning of an analysis, except to comment on the patient's varying experiences of me. I am prepared during an analysis, however, to have my interpretations rejected by the analysand, to be put forward again by me at a later time. I am mindful of Winnicott's (1941) accounts of his use of the spatula in the set situation. When he interviewed mothers and babies, sitting across the corner of a table from them, he would place a spatula between them and note the baby's relation to this important intermediate object. It had a ready potential for use, and the space between Winnicott and the infant was therefore a potential space. He found that a healthy infant would first glance at the spatula and then look away from it. He might repeat this several times. Averting his gaze constituted a 'period of hesitation' necessary to any eventual use of the actual object. Most likely, the infant uses the blank space (the area created by looking away) to give the actual object an internal status. By looking away he has the object now only in mind. He makes the object a psychic object. By rendering the object psychic, the infant links it up with the instinctual drives which have some minimal psychic representation before the use of the actual object. In this way the infant accelerates the arrival of the instincts, which – to return to Winnicott's way of looking at it – show up when his mouth opens, his cheeks go floppy, he dribbles, and his eyes focus eagerly on the actual object. This is an evolution that we can trace:

1. Perception of the actual object.
2. Creation of an internal mental space by looking away.
3. Psychic representation of the object.
4. Instincts now arrive through the internal object.
5. Holding of the internal object allows the external object to be used without anxiety.
6. The spatula is now a subjective object.

If I return to the use of interpretation by the adult analysand, it is possible to draw some comparisons between the analysis of the adult and Winnicott's presentation of the spatula to an infant. In the first place, I expect an analysand occasionally to resist interpretation of the here and now transference. Such a resistance can be the need for a period of hesitation, which is essential to the patient's own psychic rendering of the analyst and his psychoanalytic objects. After a period of hesitation a patient will usually return to the interpretation ready to use it as an object. Some clinicians might see this period of hesitation as a psychic evacuation of the transference and the analysand's temporary resistance would be interpreted. I view this as an essential feature of the introjective process, and I ordinarily do not comment on it.

The Topographic Return

As I have suggested, a psychoanalyst's interpretation of the unconscious meaning of a patient's disourse does not constitute insight. Nor indeed can we say that the analysand's subsequent references to the analyst's comments are insightful. For an analytic idea to qualify as an insight I think it must undergo **a topographic return: from the analyst's comment to a preconscious holding area (an inner mental space) where it evokes instinctual representations, unconscious affects, and unconscious memories, and then returns to consciousness after such inner work has occurred**. An analytic idea then, has been transformed into an insight because what was only a theory now bears the patient's instinctual, affective, and memorial print.

Perhaps it will be seen that this particular journey of an idea is as important a structural act as it is an educative accomplishment. The patient benefits from the psychic procedure as well as from the particular acquisition of knowledge. Many psychoanalysts have made this point but stress different elements in the endeavour. The Kleinians emphasize the way that interpretation reveals unconscious phantasies that organize the patient's location of mental contents (usually split and projectively identified) so that analytic interpretation brings together split off parts of the self. This is possible, though at times it is an intensely painful struggle, because the analyst interprets why the patient feels persecuted by this, or why the patient's elation is an effort to soar above psychic pain. Interpretation is a means of making psychic life bearable, thus enabling him to gain insight without going mad. The Kohutians stress the interpretive act as a factor in providing the patient with a self object through which the analysand evokes crucial experiences of self.

The psychoanalyst's presentation of analytical objects becomes a factor in the analysand's fulfilment of his destiny in psychoanalysis. I have said that I think the patient must be allowed a period of hesitation following certain interpretations (particularly at the beginning of analysis and whenever the analyst introduces new ideas). This allows the patient to transform the analytic idea into a psychic object by starting it on a topographic return journey, so that the idea will return informed by the patient's psychic life. As he reconsiders the interpretation, it will now be his inner object, and of use for his own subsequent production of analytical ideas.

How is a topographic return part of a destiny drive? Simply stated, the analyst has provided an object (interpretation) and a technique (allowance, without intrusion, of a period of hesitation) that enable the analysand to put the idea to complex inner use. The process itself enhances and maturates the psyche which actually 'grows' more capable of processing life through the analyst's skills. We may even claim that analysands develop a capacity, an enhanced psyche, that distinguishes them from non-analysands, although, of course, there are other people (artists, scientists, musicians, for instance) who develop elements of mind and psyche in ways not accomplished by psychoanalysis. For many people, an analyst is that object a person turns to as part of the destiny drive, to contain and process transferences, to renegotiate the terms of ego structure, and to free the true self to find its way through life experience. **The process of a topographic return, which brings a psychoanalytic object into potential use for the patient, establishes a route for the patient's true self usage of the analysis**. The essence of this employment of the analytic process is to elaborate the true self through moods, memories, and inspired ideas.

Of course, we cannot simply assume this process will occur. Some analysands cannot evolve an inner mental state through hesitation. For others, the analyst's interpretation becomes the object of an envious attack or a contemptuous diminishment. When this is so, the analyst may need to change to another psychoanalytic technique, for example, to a more dialectically confronting mode.

Varying Techniques

Psychoanalytic work must vary according to the immediate emotional reality of the session. In a single session, the analyst may need to interpret the patient's mental life in the here and now transference in order to confront the patient's destructive urges. I think of this as intensely active interpretive work, a dialectic of difference. At another moment the analyst may need to note (not interpret intensively) the patient's idealizations and loving sustaining projective identifications. The analyst should be more active when the patient, by installing his good elements into the object, leaves himself emptied of self-worth. Otherwise I think he can simply note, now and then, how the patient's love of the analyst reflects his creativity. Patients are not well served if the analyst insists that the patient's affection is entirely due to projectively identified positive qualities. An analysand rightly feels that his ability to perceive worth in the other is diminished, and that his experience of gratitude is refused. Further, this approach suggests that all object relating is simply a narcissistic circuit: the other only contains the self, and therefore affection for the other logically means only another form of love of oneself.

Then there are moments in analysis when the analyst should be uninterpretive. A patient may be lost in thought, or in preconceptions on the way to a potential realization as Bion has conceived of it, and this state of mind requires minimal analytic presence. The analyst may need to remain silent and not act on his curiosity for long stretches of time, particularly if the patient's transference state is one of ordinary regression to dependence (Bollas, 1987).

On another occasion, the analyst may need to celebrate (see chapter 4) the analysand's ego abilities, as a means of facilitating and identifying ego health as a factor in analysis and in life.

The analyst who turns to himself as an object of analysis, to analyse his previous comments as mistaken, performs yet another analytic function. This establishes a critical differential self-observing element, one that emphasizes the objective scanning of subjective life. What makes this act *objective* is the analyst's turning to himself as an object, a temporal accomplishment that can only be achieved upon reflection. The analyst who looks back on his own comments differs functionally from the analyst who associates to the patient's narrative. Analytic associating is not reflecting: it is the play of the analyst's preconscious with the patient's unconscious, and it derives from the immediate moment. Bion terms this the analyst's transformation of beta elements (in the patient and in himself) into alpha elements which then can be remembered and stored for dreaming, further associating, and eventually for psychoanalytic interpretation.

The analyst who discloses his experience of the analysand, either as an indirect expression of countertransference (Bollas, 1987) or as a direct disclosure of his state of mind, is a different object from the associating analyst. When the analyst uses his own self experience to confront the patient's pathological internal object relations, he confronts the patient by objectifying his experience in the countertransference.

And, of course, we may now add the 'classical analyst object' who sustains the analytic frame, who tends the boundary, and who keeps the value of silence as the fundamental ambience of the analysis. This is the ideal, even if some analysands can never reach it. What the neurotic patient takes for granted is an ego accomplishment for other persons. Hopefully, we analysts return to this state with our analysands in each session for significant stretches of time. Its continuous available presence (even where not active or used) is the analyst's responsibility. If an analyst is only interpretive, facilitative, celebrative, mutually playful or countertransferentially confronting, then the very core of analysis has been abandoned.

The Schools of Psychoanalysis and their Provision of Objects

It is clear, I am sure, that my view of what constitutes the analytic is not a classical or a Kleinian position. I think that each of the schools in some respects polemicizes a single feature of analytic life. Each Freudian should also be a potential Kohutian, Kleinian, Winnicottian, Lacanian, and Bionian, as each of these schools only reflects a certain limited analytic perspective.

Each of these approaches provides the analysand with a different analytic object. The Kohutian, Kleinian, Lacanian, and Bionian *objects* all potentialize a particular use of the analyst, all address a specific category of psychic movement. As such, they suggest a different element of the analysand's destiny in a psychoanalysis, as the unfolding of the true self depends on the provision and use of analytic objects. An analyst who never speaks the word 'castration', but who only uses words such as 'annihilation' fails as an object of analysand *use* to facilitate true self experiencing and knowing of the castration complex. Analysts who address a patient's positive transference through the language of 'need' and 'dependence' fail the true self need to be processed by the emotional categories represented by the words 'love', and 'erotic'. The analyst who says to a depressed female patient 'You are upset with me for leaving you this weekend, as you want mummy–me to be present all the time' is a different object serving and facilitating a totally different use function from the analyst who says to the same patient, 'You are furious with me for going home to make love to my wife when you feel that I am a fool for not doing this with you'.

Is it the case that the first interpretation or the second is correct? Is there a correct comment here? Well, certainly, one may be more correct than the other at any time, but can we ever say, of either this imaginary depressed patient, or for that matter, any patient, that either of these two comments is wrong? I don't think so. But time and again in clinical discussions one can hear a reference to a person's 'pregenital need for the analyst', or for the need to have the analyst as 'self object' which necessitates analytical language relevant to the small infant: the discourse of need, dependence, safety. But is there an adult human being alive, brain intact, whose personality is only pregenital in the sense that some oedipal sexual aims have not been experienced and represented?

Of course I am aware of the view which segments the analysand's psyche according to a kind of evolutionary libidinal flow chart, and it has a limited merit. A six-month old cannot have a six-year old's oedipus complex; time must pass. But an adult will have had an oedipus complex and oedipal desires, even if he appears to have no triangular knowledge. Even if it has been avoided by virtue of regression to a pregenital level of organization or diminished/distorted because of a fixation, he will still have had his oedipus complex. In other words, there is no adult human being with whom it is not possible meaningfully to discuss oedipal love of one parent, rivalry with the other parent, and anxiety over body mutilation. The human mind is more than sufficiently complex to embrace the seeming contradiction between a pregenital fixation and an oedipus complex occurring within the same person.

From my point of view, the contemporary analyst's task is to understand the many schools of analytic thought, as each represents a specific analytic function that needs inclusion in the psychoanalytic field (Limentani, 1986). **The psychoanalyst is an object performing multiple functions, each analyst-object being significantly more present than another analyst-object according to the clinical requirements of the analysand**. If the analyst can free himself from any freezing of his potential multiple functioning, then he can present the analysand with more usable objects within the analytic space and thereby avail the true self of more possibilities for the movement through an object as a fulfilment of its destiny.

If we understand that transference and countertransference are always linked to one another – that a transference act evokes a counter-transference state – then it is possible to note how transference always represents a particular use of an object and how the countertrans-ference also registers this use. For this intended use of an object to become available in analysis, however, the analyst must be receptive to countertransference registrations, and this understanding is akin to the development of a mental capacity (Bollas, 1987) that enables such transference use to emerge.

The Patient's Use of the Analyst's Personality

As I have suggested in chapter 1, analysands sometimes evolve the true self through use of the different parts of the analyst's per-sonality. They use the analyst's thoughtfulness, humour, sensuality, doubt, aggression, language capacity, memory, critical–interpretive ability, phantasy life, uninterpretiveness, maternal holding function, paternal presence – a list of personality elements that is virtually endless.

With the continuing interest in the transference and countertrans-ference, we psychoanalysts are more aware now not only of how we are used as an object, but also how we can understand and facilitate such use. Some years ago it would have seemed a violation of the analyst's neutrality for a clinician to have facilitated his own personality use by a patient: to feel pleasure, sadness, joy, anger, frustration, aggression, and so on – to fully experience the patient's *use* of one's self.

No analyst is ever neutral once he has met the patient. The analy-sand begins to establish himself in the analyst's mind right away. Indeed, the analyst's relaxed and receptive willingness to be used as an object if anything demonstrates a greater understanding, in my view, of the analyst's function as a blank screen. Just as a cinema screen will have a crowd of images playing across its surface, while a blank wall will not, the analyst is that screen, placed to have its blankness apparently eliminated to portray the projective world of the other. If by a countertransference we now understand a two-way projection on to this screen – from both patient and analyst – then this analytic screen represents the projective and counterprojective life of the analyst and analysand.

The analyst must not only look at the patient's feelings, word and thing presentations, but simultaneously at his own inner response. Further, as this inner response is often composed of the activation of the elements of his personality, he needs to be available for the patient's *selective use* of these elements. He needs to reconsider technique in terms of *how* to make available the dialectic of mutual use, so that the analysand will have increased understanding of himself.

To be reminded of these other elements, I shall list only a few. I focus here on what is taking place *inside* the analyst. The analyst's feeling of:

a.	contentment	j.	agitation	s.	depression
b.	pleasure	k.	aggression	t.	affection
c.	interest	l.	anger	u.	erotic response
d.	curiosity	m.	hostility	v.	love
e.	uncertainty	n.	rage	w.	quiet
f.	confusion	o.	murderousness	x.	dreaminess
g.	anxiety	p.	frustration	y.	headache
h.	alarm	q.	gloom	z.	backache
i.	irritation	r.	despair		

Each of these feelings is an element in the analyst's personality. As they are universal human elements, then the analysand, knowing this, will unconsciously use these elements in the analyst. This can involve the movement of the true self at any one moment. It moves through the use of such objects, personality elements common to us all.

Each element is not self-defining. It is often not clear initially what any of these elicited or used elements means. Any element's significance only emerges from its function within the intersubjective field. For example, one psychotic patient elicited anxiety, isolation, hate, talkative falseness, and frustration in me. What was the function of these elements at this point in the analysis? I think it was to create within me the shape of the mother's personality at the time of mothering him as an infant. As the mother was anxious, isolated, full of hate, talkative but false, and frustrated, so was I. By shaping me, the patient reconstructed his early life, a use of me that was not the free movement of true self action.

At such a moment in the analysis, I *contain* these elements in myself, and I eventually use them to pose a question: which parent (mother, father, grandparent, etc.) is he bringing out in me? He told me it was the mother, and indeed, both from the patient and, later, the mother's account, this intensely anxious, hateful state was characteristic of her during the patient's early childhood. But at another moment these very same elements (or part of them), combined with other elements of my personality, could be functioning in a different way and suggest a different meaning. For example, my senses of estrangement, fear, wordlessness, and oppression were understood by me to be the shape of the patient's personality in response to the mother's idiom of mothering.

It is, then, the types of transference that establish the function of those personality elements that comprise the countertransference.

Needless to say, these elements may be used to re-enact early object relations. A patient may use my capacity for frustration and aggression in order to engage me in a particular combat, one that involves my integration of feeling, thought, and play. Or, a patient may use my personality elements of contentment, curiosity, uncertainty, affection, quietness, and dreaminess to process the prior experience of a dream.

No two patients ever use the analyst's personality elements to achieve specific functions in the same way. Indeed, as each patient contains

1. an unconscious ego that is the structural trace of the inherited core and
2. its complex rule negotiation with the early mother, and
3. a dynamically repressed unconscious that holds the subject's private figurations of his desire

he will use analytic objects to evolve his personal idiom in that drive to articulate himself. This destiny drive is an urge to

1. elaborate the true self through experiences,
2. re-present early rules for being and relating, and
3. articulate the repressed unconscious through symbolic representations.

Perhaps I may restate a point made earlier in this book: psychoanalytic concepts are mental objects, each with its own function, and their potential presence constitutes a possible use for the analysand at any moment when he seeks to use an element to serve the true self's evolution. To the lists of the classical analytic objects, and the analyst's countertransference objects, we may add specific psychoanalytic theories which will be elicited by a patient as they come up in the analyst's mind at any one moment. I shall name a few:

a.	the oedipus complex	n.	mirroring self object	v.	black hole
b.	merger	o.	idealizing self object	w.	negative therapeutic reaction
c.	undifferentiation				
d.	symbiosis	p.	transmuting internalization	x.	death work
e.	castration			y.	*narcissisme de vie et narcissisme de mort*
f.	penis envy	q.	the law of the father		
g.	sibling rivalry				
h.	autism	r.	symbolic equation		
i.	ego ideal			z.	the transformational object
j.	superego	s.	bi logic		
k.	alpha elements	t.	transitional object		
l.	beta elements				
m.	container	u.	potential space		

These concepts are 'around' in the analyst's preconscious as a world of objects available for use by both analyst and analysand. Within reason – that is, assuming a good enough analyst – when these objects come up in the analyst's mind, they do so as a result of the patient's use of the analyst. This is one reason why I think psychoanalysis is a preferred form of treatment, compared, say, to logotherapy or Gestalt therapy. Certainly these other therapies *do* have some valuable ideas which can be used by their patients. But not enough. Not nearly enough.

I believe that a psychoanalyst (or psychoanalytic psychotherapist) is the most suitable person to treat a patient for neurotic, characterological, and psychotic problems; but it is essential for psychoanalysts to understand that theory must develop; not simply because we need to think more about psychic processes, but because we and our patients, a curious social sub-group, live within a cultural and symbolic world that is dynamic. If the world does not change for the better, it does change, and our patients speak to us in each generation in a different unconscious manner. Thus we must continuously rethink them!

Playing with the Elements

I n a sense, the patient who is using the analyst for true self passage unconsciously plays on the parts of the analyst's personality, evoking different elements to perform quite specific functions at any one time. The more elements the patient can evoke, the more he can express his own idiom. These elements, potential 'objects' that are in fact processes, are as essential to the movement of the true self as language is necessary to the speech of the subject in the Symbolic. Of course, many analysands are restricted in their evocation and use of human elements (in themselves and in the analyst) and, therefore, the analyst will analyse the defences and internal experiences that prevent the analysand's use of the object. In time the patient will develop increased element capacity, as he can use the other's personality to a greater and more varied extent. In one respect, then, psychic change can be evaluated according to the analysand's increased ability to evoke and utilize personality elements in himself and in the other. In my view, this becomes an ability to engage in play, or interplay with the other, in which each person is 'free' to associate: not simply to move spontaneously but to do so in company with an associate.

The objects an analyst provides are considerable. One thinks naturally of interpretations, or the presentation of a particular psychoanalytical concept such as the oedipus complex, but the fields of use are broadened and deepened if we include the elements of personality. By including the analyst's personality as an object of use, we bring the countertransference into the analysand's choice of object. As I have said before, there are many different transferences, so a patient will vary from session to session, or even moment to moment, in the precise transference use of a particular class of objects. For example, he may be seeking the object 'clarification' by presenting a confusion. He may seek the object 'memory' when he struggles in the analyst's presence to recall something, requesting assistance from the analyst's mnemic capability. Or he may seek the object 'silence' as he implies that he requires quiet to mull something over. He may elicit the object's 'confrontation', 'celebration', 'surprise', 'puzzlement', 'inquiry', 'reflection', 'distress', 'sadness', etc., to use such objects for the processing of an unthought known experience.

Each of these 'objects', in fact, is an experience. It involves a self state and an experience of the other. The self state is represented through the transference, as each segment of the patient's behaviour is an action within the analysis; and as it is acted on or in the presence of the psychoanalyst, there is some corresponding experience in the analyst's countertransference.

Patient and analyst are therefore continuously engaged in a mutual processing of one another. As the patient ceaselessly represents discrete needs or states of self in the transference, he requests something from the analyst. Analytical training, particularly the training analysis, gives the analyst that skill necessary to know how to respond to a patient's request for use. I suggest, however, that this skill is exceptionally complex and is underrepresented in analytical literature, perhaps because it is only fleetingly observable. It is impossible to record the discrete actions that reflect this skill. Yet it is why analysts differ from other therapists and it is what differentiates a very good analyst from a not so very good analyst.

The skill of practising psychoanalysis is in the ego processing of the patient's transference. It is in 'knowing' the predominant transference request and responding to it appropriately by providing an 'object' that serves the analysis. I think much of that skill is learned operationally through one's own analysis, and to a lesser, but still significant sense, in supervision. The budding analyst internalizes rules for being an analyst in relation to a patient through his experience in his own analysis. As the patient, he learns through this dialectic of egos (his own and his analyst's analytic ego) operational paradigms for the psychoanalytical processing of the elements of human life: phantasies, feelings, moods, thoughts, behaviours, somatic states, and so on.

As the dialectic of patient presentation (transference) and analyst processing (countertransference) is an operational segment of lived experience, each exchange is a paradigm which can become part of the unconscious ego structure of the analysand in his subsequent processing of self and other. To my way of thinking, this dialectic is not negotiated primarily by an exchange of mental representations. The analysand does not, consciously or unconsciously, mentally represent the paradigm potential of his transference segment, nor does he distil a thoughtful mental representation of the analyst's response. The transference–countertransference exchange is a dialogue of processes and is registered as an operational paradigm. Of course, patient and analyst may mentally represent the 'rule' of being and relating inherent in or following upon a transference–countertransference dialectic. And every analyst will try to think (consciously or unconsciously) before presenting an object–element to the patient, but the mental representation (what the analyst thinks to himself) is often only a part of the analyst's processing at any one moment in time of that particular transference act. Preconscious or conscious mental representation may be a derivative of the logic of the analyst's act, but the true knowledge behind the act resides in the complex grammar-like structure of the unconscious ego which co-ordinates the analytical response to the complexity of the transference act.

The Psychoanalyst's Multiple Function

The psychoanalyst's multiple function, then, refers to the analyst's *usefulness* as an object and one of these capacities is to provide those elements necessary for the elaboration of true self. I certainly do not mean an act of collusion, if by this we mean a giving in to a patient's unconscious avoidance of an issue or his search for a narcissistically terminal form of gratification.

Although the psychoanalyst enhances the movement of the true self through object usage if he can make elements of his personality available to the patient, this should be accomplished authentically. If we consider, now, the more problematic side of analytic provision of a personality element, the analyst's behaviour and interpretive stance *vis-à-vis* the patient (rather than the analyst's inner processing of the analysand), it is absolutely incorrect, in my view, to provide the patient with empathy, celebration, aggression, or even analysis, if such provision is not authentic. The patient's unconscious use of the analyst's true conviction is vital to his eventual well-being. The analyst must, then, proceed to intervene (or to remain silent) partly on the basis of his inner sense of conviction in his effort to speak the truth.

This search is a paradox. The analyst's effort to represent what is true – for the patient and for himself – is an act, simultaneously, of freedom and limitation. He is free to feel or think anything, but the effort to represent only that which feels, seems, or appears true will limit the analyst's behaviour and verbal representations. This may be so obvious that it appears hardly worth mentioning. But as I have argued both for the analyst's freedom of inner experience, and a broad use of psychoanalytic concepts, a theoretically infinite set of wordings, these elements will always be bound by the analyst's conviction which will be founded on his experience of the patient in the clinical situation.

Subject Relations Theory

The patient free associates. So does the psychoanalyst. Analysis is an interplay of two subjectivities, although the psychoanalyst has an established area of self and mind devoted to the psychic processing and interpretive knowing of the analysand. But any psychoanalytic session is a dialectic between two subjectivities, and although they will form and project internal mental representations of one another, the understanding of which we term object relations theory, they will also act in a successional interplay of idiom elements, which I think we should say is more of a subject relations theory. If object relations theory attends to the formation and projection of self and object representations, subject relations theory attends to the interplay of two human sensibilities, who together create environments unique to their cohabitation. The concepts of interplay, interrelating, intersubjectivity, have as much use in a subject relations theory as in an object relations theory.

The area between two human subjects on the verge of human dialectic is only a potential space. To become an intermediate area of experiencing, the two participants require a certain reciprocal freedom to play. Much of the work of a psychoanalysis will be devoted to enabling the patient to arrive at the point where he can be free to play in intermediate space.

A patient who is ill can attack the analysis with such skill that playing is not possible, and with some analysands such a point will never be reached, at least as a reliable accomplishment. But when the patient is at play, the analytic space is a transitional area shared by the two participants who contribute to those objects that are the creation of such play. Such objects are the patient's and analyst's verbal associations to one another, in the particular mood or environment they create. I suggest that we term any mental object (association, comment, interpretation, mood, environment, etc.) derived from patient–analyst interplay, an *intermediate object*. This respects the fact that it derives from the contribution of two subjectivities and that it is a part of the transitional dialectics of subject relations. Such objects are not transitional objects, because the transitional object is not derived from interrelating, but reflects the subject's development of his own idiom irrespective of the other's desire. An intermediate object respects the status of an object that is indeed negotiated by two subjectivities, and most analytical objects are therefore intermediate ones.

One of the psychoanalyst's functions, therefore, is to work analytically to create an intermediate area of experiencing (something not initially possible with many patients), to sustain its existence, and through continued interplay to establish through experience an intrapsychic equivalent of intermediate experiencing.

And Finally...

Perhaps it is clear that I am pleading for greater recognition in psychoanalysis of the unique idiom of each person. Although we all share elements of personality, and even live in fairly recognizable disposition groups (neurotic, borderline, psychotic), such universal elements and categories do not describe the human subject. They address the human race, that is true, but the human subject is there in a precise organization of these elements and he or she lives through this idiomatic processing of self and other.

A psychoanalysis is exceptionally suited to the analysis and facilitation of this true self idiom as the analyst who 'provides' the patient with a field of objects (elements of the analyst's personality, elements of psychoanalytical procedure, elements of psychoanalytical concepts) creates a sometimes observable universe of objects through which the patient moves. As the patient uses and organizes the objects, he may live the true self through these experiences. This form of living, however, cannot be collected into a narrative content. The true self cannot be fully described. It is less like the articulation of meaning through words which allow one to isolate a unit of meaning as in the location of a signifier, and more akin to the movement of symphonic music. But even this analogy does not do justice to the forming ephemerality of true self experience.

Each person begins life with his own true self. This is an inherited potential that comes into being through the stimulation of life experience. Each individual is unique, and the true self is an idiom of organization that seeks its personal world through the use of an object. As the person views a potential object field, he sights objects that are of interest to him, and this procedure necessitates his thoughtless discarding of certain objects in favour of objects of desire. This is true whether the person is searching for a partner, browsing in a bookshop, or listening to a symphony.

The presence of the object elicits desire. Here desire is the urge to initiate an active use of the object, whether that is to make love to the object, read the object, or listen to the object. If we take a very broad understanding of objects as phenomena that have some location, can be found and used to catalyse a particular unit of experience, then we could theoretically trace the path of the true self as reflected in the subject's choice and use of objects. Here we would include cultural objects, human objects, material objects, and so on.

The fashioning of life is something like an aesthetic: a form revealed through one's way of being. I think there is a particular urge to fashion a life, and this destiny drive is the ceaseless effort to select and use objects in order to give lived expression to one's true self. Perhaps the creativity of a human lifetime is the talent in articulating one's idiom. If the person continues to be and feel true to himself (not living compliantly) and is surprised by the continuing elaboration of his self, then he is fulfilling his destiny.

Of course, each of us is stuck at various moments in life, and some people, unfortunately, may be stuck for a lifetime, perhaps because of psychological, familial, cultural, or political circumstances. The severe retardation of true self inherent in, say, a black African's imprisonment in South Africa does not require a clinical psychoanalytical solution, but a political solution to a political problem. If a child is compelled to sequester and keep his true self hidden, as Winnicott wrote about, then as an adult he may seek a psychoanalysis.

For a very long time the analysand may create and re-create, in the transference and its countertransference, the object world that foreclosed true self elaboration. So the analysand may keep inspiring the mind of his mother *in* the analyst who may for years interpret this. Or the analysand may split and projectively identify elements of the true self and therefore have an impaired inner core, incapable of finding its true sense of life. The analyst may be engaged for some time in repairing the analysand's true self location (that is, enabling the patient to have something like an 'inner sense', or a 'gut feeling', or a 'sense of intuition').

I have found, however, even amidst the analysand's re-creation of his early object world, when I am employed to become part of a theatre, that gradually the analysand begins to use me differently. Or often there is a simultaneous other use. The patient uses elements of my personality fleetingly, for specific momentary use, in order to forge self from experience. I feel one use of me is succeeded by another, in a movement of uses, without this psychical dialectics forming itself into a story. When this is taking place, I think I am being used as an object by the patient's true self in his drive to articulate and elaborate his idiom. This is a thoughtless use of me but not one that suggests such ruthlessness is the expression of greediness or oral cannibalistic drive. On the contrary, the feeling I often have is one of pleasure at being made use of and being useful. I also feel this way when I am with my children, or as a university professor when a student seeks me out for intensive discussion of an idea he is working on.

What are the forces of destiny? As Freud argued, there is a somatic destiny that constitutes not only the fate of instincts but the illness and the particular death each of us has. There is also the force of the true self's potential which I believe becomes an urge to articulate one's idiom. There is the force of the mother/child dialectic which becomes part of the strucure of the ego, a logic that partly informs the fate of man's object choices and self experience.

Do we become the bearer of our destiny? Hopefully, at least in part, we all have a sense of how we have not articulated an aspect of our idiom. I think, for example, that my true talent was probably in musical composition, but I do not play an instrument. Fate and the unavailability of objects perhaps contributed to this failed articulation. But equally, I know I have nothing 'in' me that could find its elaboration through being an engineer or a computer scientist. A baseball player in adolescence, I was tempted to try for major league ball, and I have a kind of 'phantom limb' relation to the future self (as baseball player) that I never became. I can feel the trace of the gestures and experiences of my body self into a future that never materialized, and I miss that extension of myself.

The forces of destiny require an object world prepared for its use, and a child can only elaborate his idiom through those objects provided for him by the parents. A good enough mother and father have some inner sense of those objects a child can use, and the talent of parenting is to provide the correct object. This is less thought about than it is intuitively known, and a parent's attunement to the child will largely determine whether this child's evolution will be a fulfilment of his destiny (true self) or whether it will be seemingly dictated by the interventions of fate (false self). A child will be likely to have a sense of destiny if it is his fate to have good enough parents, but he will only have a schizoid sense of fate and fatedness if the parent mucks up the parenting. To be the object of the fates is another way of talking about being the object of parental injunction.

A person who meets up with a parent who is a good enough transformational object will have a sense of hope built into object use, as the paradigm-forming early object relations have resulted in important transformations in the infant's state. Perhaps this is why a person has a sense of destiny, a sense that he is elaborating his core self through life experience. It is the mother/infant relationship that provides this sense.

Is not one pleasure of loving and being loved the realization that one is truly known? In some ways is it not more important to be known by a partner than to be loved, if we mean by love that intensity of feeling that occurs when two people are falling for each other? And is not this act of falling some kind of deep affection for the precise idiom of the other: for the way the other walks, sits, smiles, talks, expresses feelings? When in love is it not the small or undramatic and precise features of the other that are so important – the way the other uses the hands to gesture, the way the other arranges ordinary objects, the way the other views the world in small and distinctive ways?

In other words, to love and to be loved is an act of deep appreciative knowing, even if much of this knowing is resistant to verbal transformation. Infants, children, adolescents, and adults need this kind of love in order to fulfil that destiny that is an articulation of their inner potential. A mother loves her infant's *precise* nature, and she works to meet this idiom, to give the infant what he needs to be himself. Maternal care, then, is a knowing that is an act of love, and whether we are to have our right to a destiny or whether we are to have a fate will, in my view, depend on whether a mother can love her infant in a knowing way.

Maternal knowing derives from the mother's capacity to sense her baby's true self and to find ways to elicit the infant's potential articulations. By articulation I mean not only the statements of personality, the expressions of character, but equally, his early verbalizations. The evolution, then, of the true self depends on the mother's transformational skills and each human subject's sense of characterological ability – the talent to live – will partly derive from his mother's understanding of his idiom. (And of course mothers will vary in their ability according to different children.) The subject's drive to elaborate his true self, then, takes him to the object world, and objects are an intrinsic part of the potential elaboration of the true self. If we think of a psychoanalysis, it is accurate to say that when the analysand uses the elements of the analyst's personality through which to move and articulate a potential, that the analyst's skill (like the mother's transformational process) is a significant pathway for the subject's articulation of himself. One of the forces of destiny in a psychoanalysis, then, resides in the intelligent use potential of the analyst, enabling him to become part of the elaboration of his analysand's true self.

Part Two

6

The Ghostline Personality

The theory of the transitional object has helped us to think about the infant's transition from a partly hallucinated wish world to the creative use of actual objects in the service of the child's desire. This is not simply a matter of cognitive development: we know that the neonate is capable of perceiving features of the actual world. It is a question of the infant's *psychic* evolution, which is forged through the illusion (facilitated by the mother) that the actual world is formed according to the infant's need, and that reality creates itself out of his wishes. This illusion permits the psyche to develop in the way it usually does where, for example, phantasy plays such an important part in this evolution.

The psychoanalysis of psychotic children and adults is often concerned with a person's failure in infancy to make a transition from hallucinated thought to the creative use of actual objects in the service of self and others. Some children do not achieve this, and the autistic child is a haunting witness to this failure. One of the psychoanalytic world's gifted theoreticians on autism, Frances Tustin (1981), has defined the object that such a child uses as an autistic one. It is not employed to fulfil its intended function, such as a key being played with to open or unlock doors, but is utilized as an asymbolic sensation-producing 'thing', such as when a key is knocked about because it is hard.

An object is transitional according to the infant's particular use of it. A child may employ an object in an intense manner. He may even have it with him much of the time, but if this use of the object is outside the transitional space or the intermediate area of experiencing, then it is not a transitional one. A transitional object signifies an intervention between the purely internal world and the 'thingness' of actual objects. The object can be used in this way only if a potential space has been created by that maternal care that sponsors the infant's use of illusion. If the mother cannot facilitate this potential space, the infant's true self will not evolve through the creative use of objects, and he will not discover the third area of human experiencing.

A schizoid solution would be to split the self by creating a pathological divide between the true and the false self. The true self remains hidden, lives in phantasizing or daydreaming, where it may be said to have an alternative life.

The Alternative Object

I think it may be useful to consider a particular use of objects that is to be found along the schizoid path. I refer to those children who turn away from transitional objects in order to foster alternative objects. The child silently refuses to use the actual object world (of persons and cultural objects). This schizoid development involves an appropriation of objects (actual and mental) to construct a special inner mental space (Stewart, 1985) that becomes an alternative world. The alternative object, if actual, is used as if it has no psychosomatic meaning. It is not loved and hated. It is not passionately enjoyed as is the transitional object. The alternative object expresses the child's sense of the death of transitional life, of the collapse of potential space, and the movement toward the compensatory construction of an alternative inner world, far removed from the actual.

This alternative area differs from the internal world proper, in that the objects that are transported to this region, or created there, have a special presence to them; a uniquely alternative object world, alternative even to ordinary inner space. I think these inner objects achieve this special presence, because they are the afterlife and personify the spirits of the dead. The dead here represent the death of self states or others (Green, 1983) and of futures.

For reasons that I hope will become clear, I propose that we recognize this special inner area as bounded by a ghostline. **When the subject passes an object representation across this inner line, he deliberately alters it and defines it as a unique inner presence.** In particular, he has a sense of creating something else out of the actual object world, of spiriting the essence of self and other states to this alternative world, where former self and others live on like spirits or ghosts. It is not like an internal object proper that represents an actual other. When this person thinks of others or objectifies the self, these internal objects reflect the anguish of this person's frame of mind, while the objects beyond the ghostline are fundamentally transformed into traces of actual objects that feel more within the control of the subject.

I think the inner objects are ghostly because they are the remains of the body–self, and preserve the spirit of formerly meaningful psychosomatic existence.

We are now in a position to make the following comparison:

Transitional Object	–	Alternative Object
Potential Space	–	Fated Space
Transitional Space in the Third Area	–	Alternative Space beyond the Ghostline
Use of the Object	–	Conservation of the Object

I shall now turn to clinical vignettes to provide a further sense of what I am trying to discuss.

Jeff

In the 1960s I worked at a day school for autistic children in Oakland, California. I was employed as a 'teacher-counsellor' which meant that I was responsible for teaching simple tasks and some school work to autistic, schizophrenic, and very disturbed children. In fact, very little 'academic' work could be done, as one was inevitably involved in doing psychotherapy. It was my privilege to work with one child who had just begun speaking shortly before I came to the school. He was nine years old, quite hefty and rotund, and he tended to 'think himself out' by acting. If he was cross with another child, he would approach the offender, state his grievance, ceremonially allow the child's verbal or silent response, and then, in any event, either pummel, spit at, kick, or strangely 'forgive' the child. All depended on what he thought.

One of my tasks was to find some way to help him through this expression of his internal life, and my colleagues all shared a certain urgent need for this patient to improve as their shins were sore, and their clothing bills had risen since his mud-throwing and spitting had increased. In the course of time I found that Jeff liked a story I told him. It occurred to me one day when he was involved in writing his umpteenth comic book, in which he portrayed members of the school and sent them to horrid deaths. Some of the other children, who were uncertain about the difference between a representation of them and their actual selves, were terrified every time Jeff put them in one of his comic books. So I said, 'Come, let me tell you about an orange ship, which goes around the world'. He liked stories, orange was his favourite colour, and he could occupy himself with maps for hours on end. He made me the captain of the ship, appointed himself first mate, and his schoolmates were given differing assignments on board.

Typically, I would make the ship stop in an interesting port of call, such as Alexandria. This would satisfy my need to create some educational dimension, as I could use this moment to talk about the history and customs of another country. I would usually accomplish this through the captain's lecture to his crew before anyone disembarked. Then Jeff would take over and immediately tell me that one child had fallen in the water, another had been eaten by a lion, or a third had been run over by a bus. As he said this his eyes would light up, he would shake his hands, sometimes jump about in his seat, and roar with a kind of nervous laugh. I would reply, 'No, Jeff that's not what happened', and I would rescue any victims, and send them on to better fates. Jeff would cry out, 'No, no, that's not what happened', and he would wait for me to finish before giving his alternative account.

After a year or so of this, I had many occasions to wonder about the wisdom of this procedure. The story assumed an increasing significance in his life until finally, as he would enter the school gates in the morning, he would scream out with glee, 'The orange ship! The orange ship!' and I set a particular time of day to work on the story with him. I wondered if I were simply colluding with his search for an alternative world, but my colleagues said that they thought it was a good thing because it involved two people, because his violence toward the other children had lessened, and because they were encouraged by his tolerance of my version of the world. Then one day, after the orange ship journey, when he had murdered quite a few children, and I had earnestly revived them he said, 'You don't get it!' I didn't know what he was talking about. He then ran all over the school saying, 'Chris Ball [his name for me] does not get it!' and it was some time before he could settle down to tell me what I did not get. He said, 'I'm *joking*. I'm joking', and he told me that he had been making up dire events for some days to see if I knew that he really didn't mean what he said. For another two weeks we continued the orange ship journeys and Jeff would tell me his versions of the story, now amused that I could think this was what he intended.

In some respects Jeff used the orange ship as an object of transitional use, and my representation of fictional happenings matriculated elements of the actual world into this potential space, while he represented his fantasy life. My work was not that of an analyst (I was a college graduate and this was well over my head) but, in reflecting on my work with Jeff, I have occasion to dwell on his transition from schizophrenic fantasying to the use of cultural objects.

Paul

There were other children who did not accomplish this transition. Paul, for example, was the master comic-book writer. Hunched over his desk, scowling or roaring with laughter, he lived in order to populate his books. His cast of characters, to some of whom he had given fictional life for five years, were very important to him. It would not be true to say that he was completely cut off from the other children in the school. Indeed, he often had a crowd of admirers surrounding him and he enjoyed his status as the master of comics. And although Jeff was something of a chum, Paul played with him as if Jeff were inside a comic book. He signified this by occasionally tapping Jeff on the top of his head with his index finger, and he would hum while doing this. Those of us who knew him well of course understood that he was 'writing' the entire scene. Indeed this scripting of life gave him a lot of pleasure and now and then, when Paul would actually look at me (he usually looked just slightly off to the side of a person), his eyes would gleam and I knew I was just then being processed and stored for comic book usage.

Mary

I stopped working with children, pursued graduate studies in English literature and simultaneously received a psychotherapy training, the patients being university students. One patient in particular reminded me of Jeff and Paul. Mary was an exceptionally gifted philosophy student who felt suicidal. I discovered that along with two female friends she lived in a pretend alternative world. They had created their own private language (more complex than back slang), had invented names, and discussed purely imaginary characters who constituted a kind of ongoing soap opera. They had a group name, dressed exactly alike, and were almost inseparable. Indeed, I saw the other two members of the trio after Mary insisted that she could not continue with me until they had talked to me. I said I thought that this must be so they could invent my imaginary twin and thus establish me as one of their collective persons. Mary, however, had sought me out because she was in fact deeply worried by their secret society. She did not put it to me that way. Instead, she came to talk about one of them who worried her. She saw her as perhaps too powerful, and she illustrated how this other student exercised a very cruel control over the third member of the trio. I sensed that Mary wanted to be out of this all, but she was frightened that she would be seriously harmed if she tried to free herself from this other girl's grasp. Indeed, at the time of her self-referral, she was getting deeper into the practice of witchcraft, and had startled, and I think offended, a teacher by apologizing for being late one day on the grounds that her flight had been late. She was not referring to planes.

Eventually Mary was able to leave her curious friends, and understand how their group provided her with a collective alternative to her lonesome life at home. Mary's sharing of a pretend alternative world with her friends was, in my view, an effort to emerge from intense isolation as a child into a type of ritualized oral narrative as a precursor to play. I believe she had transported self and other objects beyond the ghostline as a child and had lived with these inner presences by transforming them into characters (as *alter* selves and *alter* others). At university she enacted this process and thus achieved a meaningful symbolic presentation of it.

Adrienne

Ten years later I met another patient for an analysis, who had been cultivating an alternative life. Since early childhood she had developed an *alter* self, a 'princess' figure, who lived on an alien planet, and who was a very powerful figure in a feudal-type society. She was admired for her beauty, intelligence, and power. The daughter of a good king who had been murdered by his brother, she and her uncle lived on opposite sides of the planet, and engaged in countless intrigues and wars against one another.

Adrienne had cultivated this alternative world since childhood, and it had a complex history after some twenty-five years of existence. Her main characters were still existent and had aged in accord with her development. The princess had originally been a child but was now an adult woman. Adrienne would take people from her life and put them in her world, although their representation of an actual person faded out as they became more autonomous.

A perfectly ordinary looking woman who had a respectable job, Adrienne was referred to analysis for a depression occasioned by harsh words said to her by a senior colleague. The referring therapist considered her suicidal. I shall not give an account of her analysis, except to emphasize some elements relevant to my focus. She had acquaintances but few friends. Her most intense experiences with people had been affairs with men, but this waned in the last years prior to her analysis. The affairs were intensely sexual but strangely personless, although she felt close to one man who had treated her quite badly, so far as I could tell.

She lived her life according to a set routine. After work she would take the bus home where she would prepare a meal, have a bath, and then read fiction. She read partly to pass the time, partly because it was intrinsically pleasurable, but mostly because she like the alterity (see p. 130) of fiction. She felt comfortable 'there'. It was the place where she lived. It was also a valued source of material for her own alternative world.

No matter where she was, this alternative world was always with her. She thought of it as a parallel world. Sometimes when thinking to herself she would address herself as 'she'. On occasion, it was a persecuting form of address, but it was also an indication that this other self, the princess, was always there. Sometimes when she looked at herself internally she 'saw' the princess.

She did not tell me about her other life until well after the first year of analysis. She did allude to the significance of daydreaming and reading fiction, but I did not know of her parallel life. Her sessions were occupied with intense and distressed accounts of work. She felt deeply persecuted by colleagues. It became clear that the essence of the persecution was not to be found in the environment, in the context of criticisms, or in the psyche, derived from any destructive attack on colleagues. Rather she simply had no idea what to do or to say when criticized. She felt absolutely incapable of acknowledging her colleagues, and this irritated them. On the other hand, she worked exceptionally hard at her job, which was technical, and her workmates allowed her to be alone as much as possible.

Adrienne's construction of a parallel world was no mystery. Her descriptions of her mother were at times even painful to hear. Mum lived in a fog; absent-minded and daydreamy, she nattered on and on about anything that crossed her mind. She talked to Adrienne about Adrienne as if she were dreaming Adrienne in Adrienne's presence. Often Adrienne would be privately furious over her mother's assumptions about her, about her hundreds of ideas about what Adrienne was thinking at just that moment.

If we think of the mother as the guarantor of the child's successful use of the transitional object, we could say that Adrienne refused transitional object usage because she did not want to enter into her mother's provisional world. Indeed, her mother related to Adrienne as if she were only an internal object, which Adrienne mirrored by transporting the actuality in her construction of objects into a deeply sequestered internality. Was Adrienne a figure in the mother's soap opera? Was she first a ghost before she constructed her own world of ghosts?

The Ghostline Personality

Jeff, Mary, and Adrienne have given me occasion to ponder the nature of this kind of person's use of the object. Jeff's use of the orange ship story suggested the capability of employing a transitional object. Mary's weird make-believe world of witches and her participation in the strange trio also indicated an effort to move the purely internal world into external reality. And Adrienne's lifelong soap opera was certainly an effort to mix reality with dream, even though it was part of her separation from the actual world.

But Adrienne established an alternative world complete with *alter* selves and others that was profoundly refusing of the actual world. There was something ghostly about these internal objects – we could say Adrienne was a ghostline personality. What do I mean by this?

If these internal objects are derived from living people (including the person's self), then they are rather like the common notion of a ghost as the spirit of that which has lived. The person feels that the object is almost alive or real and has a continuing personality presence. He believes that he has a special nurturing relation to the ghosts so that their existence depends on his survival.

Although it seems a fanciful way to talk about a schizoid situation – to say that alternative objects are psychic ghosts – I think such hyperbole accentuates the mental status of these inner presences. Above all, it stresses the fact that these objects have lived before in some state and now exist as traces of the original. Jeff felt, in quite a psychotic way, that he was putting actual people on the orange ship. That's why there was such joy for him in joking about it. He managed to differentiate between actual and internal objects. Mary and her friends populated a world that they collectively pretended to be actual though they partly believed that their fictional characters were summoned from some strange and mysterious place. When they saw someone in the actual world whom they liked or disliked, they would often agree that this person was in fact a transformation of one of their imagined characters, and they would then designate the person as such. Adrienne was very reluctant to put someone from the real world into her parallel world. When they did go there, it was only after meticulous scrutiny. I think this was because she felt she had to keep the ghost alive in the ongoing drama. I am unaware of any of these figures ever being terminated, even though someone might disappear for long periods of time.

Susan

A Swedish patient, Susan, was in her late fifties when she began once-weekly psychotherapy. She complained of feeling depressed, but her manner was almost wilfully cheerful. She was a highly successful business executive, very smart, charming, and quick witted, but she had ceased to have a sexual life with her husband, and though she admired him, she felt ignored by him, and as a consequence she was furious. She came from the country and was raised by an overly sensitive alcoholic mother and an indifferent father who favoured her elder sister.

After working with Susan for a few months, I mentioned that as yet she had carefully avoided any reference to her sexual life. 'That's right!' she smiled, suggesting that she wasn't about to tell me. She then said, 'I don't have any, really' and blushed. She meant that she didn't have any erotic fantasies about her husband, but she had been living an erotic life for some years with different film characters. Robert Redford had been a lover, and she would daydream that he was watching her in a lovingly admiring way while she was going about her ordinary household tasks. In her early fifties her imaginary life became so intense that she diminished it, and it was clear that this is when she became depressed. She had felt that her daydreams were interfering with her life.

She was an exceptionally proud woman who was not a natural for psychotherapy. She much preferred to talk about business life rather than discuss her inner world, and it was hard going for some months. With rather endearing scepticism, she brought dreams to the sessions, because this is what she had seen at the cinema. Then one week she told me that she had been on a trip with her husband, and while with him in the car she had been imagining life with one of her lovers. She was quite embarrassed and did not want to discuss it in any detail. I said that I knew that she found her husband's attention to her insufficient, and she recollected that she had begun daydreaming when she was upset with him for not understanding something she was saying to him. The next time I saw her she proudly said that she had had two dreams and a quarrel with her husband. In the first dream she is driving a car down a road that leads to her father's house. As they park the car, it tilts over gently on to its side and she is not hurt. Then she and the person whom she is with drive off. The most salient part of the dream is that she knows she is not driving the car, and therefore she must be with someone, but there is no representative of him or her. The dream occurred on the night following the session with me in which she told me of driving with her husband. Her associations to the dream were to her father's car and her father's habit of forgetting to put the brake on which meant the car rolled now and then. She also thought of her cousin who lives with her father and who is a recovered alcoholic.

The argument with her husband was while they were in the sitting-room. She was in the process of telling him about a detail of her work life when he said that she had already told him this before. She felt very cross with him for his abruptness and, characteristically, went silent.

That night she dreamed that she was at home alone, and, as she was walking from one room to the next, she saw a woman through the window. This figure, clad in a red ice-skating outfit, was holding a gun. Susan yelled out the name 'Rudolpho!' and dived to the floor just as the woman fired.

Susan was particularly amazed by this last dream and repeated it with mixed embarrassment and glee. So what can possibly be done with this, she wondered. She was especially perplexed by why she would call for Rudolpho, as she hardly knew him. She had no interest in him and had met him at only a few social dinners. She could not understand the dream.

I evoked the presence of her good humour to say, 'Now, come on! You are in a house, a woman in red shoots at you, and you call out a man's name: what does that suggest to you?' She chuckled and said it seemed to be now quite obvious. But she still did not understand it because she was alone in the house. There was no Rudolpho there, so why had she cried out for him? I said, 'Rudolpho was not there as an actual person, but he was there as an imaginary lover'. I then said I thought this dream was about her wish to transform an imaginary lover into a real person, and the dream was a response to her husband's dismissal of her. Distressed by the actual object she 'went' to her lover, and it was characteristic of her to move immediately to her imaginary world when suffering a disappointment. She nodded uncomfortably. The first dream derived from our last session, I said, so that her companion in the car was the not–there man, the imaginary figure. Why should it be her father's car and his house? Because I thought that the dream crystallized a memory of the origins of her imaginary lovers. She found her father's indifference distressing and went off into the world of daydreams to find a father who would love her. She became quite tearful and asked me why her cousin was in the dream and after discussing her cousin with her, it was clear that she imagined the cousin to have had a better, 'intoxicated', relationship to her father, who could leave the brakes off, and so the not unpleasant rolling over in the car seemed to me an erotic moment with her father.

Imagining is essential to human life. There is nothing intrinsically pathological about the imaginary creation of a lover, of an ongoing serial, but in persons whom I designate ghostline personalities, I do think we can say that the imaginary is overexploited to compensate for true disappointments in the actual world. Each person above – Jeff, Mary, Adrienne and Susan – felt altered by one or both of the parents when they were small children. They felt marginalized, fated to be alternative to the true self. Life seemed to put them beyond the ghostline, so they experienced themselves as the semi-corporeal realizations of the parents' inner objects, and in turn, experienced their true self as a phantom of what could have been.

Adrienne organized this fate into a recurring theatre. She implicitly accepted her ghostliness as an actual person, and tended to dress in black or sombre colours which I thought expressed her mourning for the lost self. Susan had married and was much more confident than Adrienne. Her sponsorship of an alternative world was a less radical act than Adrienne's. Adrienne had given herself over to it. She was quite de-skilled by virtue of her withdrawal. Susan's lovers were erotically pleasing figures, and she was depressed at the ending of this imaginary relation. Adrienne's entire life was to be found 'there'. Since early childhood she processed her existence through the imaginary world. Susan's lovers were figures who compensated for the absence of that early father who was still part–mother.

Is it possible to differentiate an imaginary from a ghostline world? Certainly the alternative world would have to be a form of imagination. Can we allocate it a special status? I think so. The mental objects that populate this imaginary world have a ghost-like status. Although they do not actually exist, the subject cathects them as if they were half alive. Indeed the subject comes more alive in relation to the ghosts than he does to actual persons. This is a transfer of life, a transformation of libido from the self and others to the figures that populate the alternative world. When the imaginary object becomes enlivened by a continuous transfer of the life instincts from the actual world to the imaginary, then I think we can say that the subject has crossed the ghostline, an inner boundary in the internal world, a reversed 'beyond', where the internal object lives off the de-cathexis of an actual other. Its ghostliness is partly due to the fact that it derives from a death, but its presence is generated by an economic borrowing of psychic energy rather than a mirorring of actual others.

This alternative object 'world' is a different place from the 'world' we refer to when we speak of an inner object world. The inner world is permeable and allows for an intercourse with the actual world through projections and introjections. It exists midway between the unconscious and perception of the actual, and objectifies the claims of both the purely internal and the external. The ghostline world is a sequestered inner space that is effected by a wilful and conscious control of the ghosts that inhabit it. Of course, the characters and plots that are hatched and developed owe much to unconscious choice, but the person does not surrender to the unconscious or use the unconscious in the way that he does ordinarily. Adrienne, for example, did have an internal world that was permeable, that reflected the actual world and expressed her instinctual life. Her mental representations of colleagues, friends, family, and me reflected the dynamic features we are accustomed to in considering the internal world. But the ghostline world is denuded of a meaningful interplay between the areas of the mind that process internal and external reality. As such, the person maintains an inner distance from the world. It is a playless space. Usually stylized and ritualized, it is a location for the safe placement of dead selves, a kind of haunted graveyard.

The Ghostline Transference

This understanding has helped me to think about the particular nature of the transferences of such persons. There is one moment in the treatment of the ghostline personality that needs mentioning. When the patient exports energy from the ghosts to the sessions, or imports energy from the analyst to vitalize the ghost world, it gives the session a very peculiar atmosphere. Such a moment is like a seance. At times the patient is clearly 'elsewhere', and the voice speaking to the analyst about the stuff of life is clearly on automatic pilot as the person is really quite gone. The analyst is, then, left with a ghost.

When the patient decides to tell the analyst about his ghosts, the telling is unlike any other narrative I have heard. It is not simply a reporting to the analyst. It is an effort to transport the object to the consulting room. The person's affiliation with the ghosts is in the form of a hidden object-relating. Again this clearly distinguishes the quality of these alternative figures from ordinary internal objects. They are meant to be secret: the person's relation to them is like keeping a lover. The revelation of the secret is worrying, much like a patient's disclosure of a secret affair is distressing.

Invariably the person fears that disclosure to an analyst will terminate the relation to the objects. Thus in telling the analyst about the ghosts, these patients often simultaneously reassure the ghosts that all is well, even in the telling. Adrienne was tenaciously protective of the integrity of each object's character. The mood she went into as she introduced me to her ghosts was one of, 'Now this silly actual man must be told about you, but don't you fear, just as soon as I have satisfied his need to know about you, I will put you back exactly where I left you, and nothing will be different'. I noticed that she could not (or would not) elaborate on any of her ghosts. She refused to free associate to them, and then she indicated that they were only what they were and that she did not want to muddle her inner world by imagining something about one of the characters in her sessions with me, because this would start the story in the wrong place (between her and me) and she wanted to keep this a world apart.

Aetiological Considerations

As I have suggested, the schizoid path taken by the child who develops a relation to these ghosts is an act of *alterity*. The child chooses to live in an alternative, purely internal world, rather than to negotiate a settlement with the actual life of the family, peers, and others. I would not suggest that there is a single route to this selection, but I think we can consider at least three fundamentally different but nonetheless related pathways to this schizoid solution.

In the first situation the child does not feel right in his soma or his own body. Indeed the soma seems to be a register of instinctual attack, and the body a clumsy outcome of erogenous zones. The child establishes an anti-libidinal defence against the psychic pains caused by instinctual pressures in the soma, and the narcissistic view of the body as an object. The late Paula Heimann suggested to me that those persons who have not received the positive cathexis of their somatic processes and bodily presence by the mother experience instinctual needs and the body as an alien phenomenon, thus bearing some feature of the mother's attitude in their own relation to themself as an object (Bollas, 1987). This child, then, projects the experience of instinctual precariousness and bodily alienation into the imaginary setting which is peopled by characters who personify such self states.

A somewhat different route is taken by a child who feels altered by the mother's specific characterizations of him. In this situation the child sets up a silent and secret *alter* self that sustains some true self life. This alternative world competes with the mother's system of representations, but the antithetical nature of such alterity is suffused with a mournful and enraged hostility that achieves plentiful representations in the figures who populate this inner world. As the mother has aimed (in this child's experience at least) to change him to suit her, he transfers the essence of this process (and its resistance) into a fraught world of inner objects that express the terms of this relationship.

A third choice, biased by a slightly different set of circumstances, occurs when the child experiences the mother as fundamentally 'dead' (Green, 1987). In her own right she is a ghost, and her lifelessness is such that the child cannot transform the libidinal cathexis of a transitional object into a life principle, into that assumption, achieved through transitional object usage, that there is an intermediate space between the self and other that makes creative living possible. For this child it would mean living with the dead, so he turns to alternative objects that then reflect the transfer of despair and resourcelessness into this world.

I expect there are other reasons for such alternative object choice. It is important when considering such persons to bear in mind that the internal objects that become alternative to self–other life reflect the character of the child's experience of the mother. In all of these cases, however, the child chooses alterity in order to create a space for some true self existence, but unfortunately, the ghostline world testifies to the existential deaths of potential self states, ones which are now only to have a psychic representation. The ghostline world, then, is a cemeterial space, a 'final resting place' for those selves that inevitably reflect the character of their deaths.

The Internal Emotional Climate

Perhaps this sequestration of the true self helps us to understand something of the subject's relation to this alternative world. I find that patients are protective of the *alter* selves and *alter* objects that populate this place. Indeed, at times they can be so dominated by such figures that it's difficult to imagine them being in charge; it is as if they 'give in' to these figures in order to keep them alive. Is it possible that the night-time life of the vampire person testifies to the function of the dream in sustaining the character–presence of such self states? Certainly one can be reminded of the nature of the dream experience when thinking of the ghostline world, as the subject dwells in a place where objects are not so much represented as they are lived. This living of the inner objects is one of the intriguing accomplishments of the imaginative, and the pervasive use of this form of alterity differentiates the schizoid person who forms a ghostline area from the individual who is a 'blank self' (Giovacchini, 1972), an 'anti-analysand' (McDougall, 1980), or a 'normotic personality' (Bollas, 1987).

Even if the cultures of the ghostline world may be permeated by violence, by grief, or by reparative scenarios, it is a space which, to the subject, feels like a contained presence, a psychic womb that nurtures a potential life. In this respect the subject feels as if he not only nourishes these *alter* selves and objects, but incarcerates them as well. The incarcerating womb, the retrospective foetalization of self states, captures something of the process of reversal, the anti-developmental character of this process. For there is an intense refusal to allow any of these inner objects to come into existential being. That is, they are secrets of the person, not to be acted out through the subject's behaviour, as signatures of his personality, but to be acted in.

Therefore there is a fundamental intrapsychic precariousness produced by the subject's determination to split off these selves and keep them internal. In a sense, this continuous killing of the selves sponsors an unconscious fear that the ghostly inhabitants of this space will one day break out and take their revenge upon the host. Can we think here of the vampires who seem always on the verge of destroying their own Dracula?

At the extreme we have a paranoid schizophrenia where the internal objects break out in the subject's hallucinated state. The schizophrenic no longer feels himself to be a creator of the alternative world but a keeper of powerful objects that will dominate him. One schizophrenic patient was convinced of the independent presubjective status of his hallucinations. He would show me paintings with some of these creatures floating about: ghostly traces of potential selves. He was certain they existed before man, that they were phylogenetic memories of the presence of space creatures who preceded and authorized him.

His deep conviction about their power brings me to another feature of the child's creation of the ghostline world. I think the power of a child's despair, or murderous feelings, or fear informs the mood of this inner world. It is a double transfer of affect: first, from the experiencing subject to an other (a ghost); second, from an emotional state to a character who personifies this state. So the ghostline world is also populated by allegorized feelings.

The intensity of feelings that drive a child to re-situate the true self into an alternative space becomes the emotional climate of this world. It is, then, a strange kind of inner hell, and this, to my mind, is the reason why we cannot sanguinely say of such persons' inner life, 'Yes, but it's simply an imaginary world, which is of course not pathological'. Indeed, it is a profound accomplishment of such persons that they can create this inner hell (even if it's an idealized version of it – a heaven) and yet preserve the true self as a potential. The image that comes to my mind is of an abortion that includes the womb, a psychic act where the womb sustains the foetus but is entirely cut off from the rest of the world. It is an inner space, in which the true self is only a potential, where there is little elaboration or articulation of personal idiom, only repetitions and variations on repetitions of the existential experiences of the true self.

The Dying of the Transitional Object

The child who moves a part of the self across the ghostline into an alternative world experiences the corporeal-like death of this self. It is as if he has handled the transitional object, has felt and experienced the pleasure of its actuality, and at the moment of imaginative use, the object dies in his grasp. It gives up its life. It makes a transition to no place. This, of course, is because the mother no longer facilitates the child's elaboration of idiom. This de-cathexis of an object, terminated by its spiritless potential, is the death of the essence of object usage and relating. In this death of essence the object gives up its spirit, gives up its ghost, which the child captures and tries to seal within a deep inner space which contains other ghosts. The death of the essence of object usage can result in the 'ghostification' of the self and its objects: a transfer into alterity.

At the same time as the transitional object loses its essence, a part of the child's psycho–somatic living dies, and this loss of a psycho–somatic experiencing is transferred into the objects beyond the ghostline who have the status of an inner presence that is the psychic trace of former psycho–somatic living. At this moment in my writing I came across a passage from Winnicott: 'the wholeness of personal integration brings with it the *possibility* and indeed the *certainty of death*; and with the acceptance of death there can come a great relief, relief from fear of the alternatives, such as disintegration, or ghosts – that is the lingering on of spirit phenomena after the death of the somatic half of the psychosomatic partnership' (1968, p. 61, author's italics).

The ghostline world could be seen as this 'lingering on of spirit phenomena', and the person's sense of containing a presence registers the particular history of these inner objects, which are different in quality from most other mental representations, because they bear the trace of a prior psychosomatic life.

Certainly some people's belief in re-incarnation must be based on dis-incarnations which impel the subject to aim for a re-incarnation, a re-embodiment into psycho-somatic integrity. The concept of transformations from the body to another body is specific to the schizoid passage of the ghostline person who is cumulatively dis-incarnated by maternal failure. I think another expression of this need for cure is found when people undergoing a faith healing feel the laying on of hands as transformative, an alteration that gives to the seeker a form of love not present, perhaps, in the mother's laying on of her hands.

The sense of being taken out of one's existence, of one's removal to an alternate world, may give this person a certain attitude to psychic transportation, a belief that he can also reverse this process and move into actual object settings without matriculative labour. He can step right in, or so he thinks. The failure of the actual world to support this idea of self-transportation is often experienced as a bewildering surprise.

Alternatively, such people come to believe that as persons they are not present, or are only partly visible. As so much of the true self has been spirited off elsewhere, they do not feel their existence is sufficiently real for the other to cathect them as an object. They can be shocked when someone falls in love with them or holds them responsible for their behaviour. I could see Adrienne struggle in considerable confusion to try to transform a new-found lover into the spiritual world of the ghostline. She tried to accomplish this by changing the terms of their relationship, which I shall describe in brief to illustrate the nature of her effort. Adrienne is an attractive woman, and while lying on a beach in a scanty bathing costume a young man fell for her. He asked her for dinner, they went for romantic walks together, and after a few days of lovemaking the young man pledged his love to her and said he wanted to see more of her. She was quite drawn to his courtship until his proposal which suggested to her that he wanted to continue the relationship. At this point she did not know what to do with him. What could she do? Where was she to put him? He was all right as a handsome object on the beach, but as an actual person to live with through time, how could she do this? So she gradually changed her voice when with him. She addressed him in tones of externalized subvocalization, as if she were talking to one of her ghosts. I gather from her accounts that initially he took this to be an endearing voice, the utterance of a kind of baby talk, until he understood that she insisted in speaking to him only from this position. She also ceased direct eye contact with him and began to knit him a jumper and to buy him small objects such as a book or a comb with which she somewhat surrounded him. I think she was transforming a living person into a purely psychic object, an act of ghostification because it was only as a ghost that he could be found. In any event, after a few days the young man concluded that she was mad and left the beach, apparently wiser but shattered.

Eviscerative Projective Identification

The person whom I am describing has a curious relation to actual others, including, of course, the analyst. I must make a seemingly nonsensical statement to describe the nature of their projective and introjective processes: the subject projects feelings and ideas through the others into an alternative beyond. This projective process eviscerates the essence of the other solely for projective purposes. Thus these projective identifications do not enhance the subject's experiential understanding of the other, who contains the projective identifications. The subject projects a part of himself into a segment of the other's personality which is quickly spirited into the secluded alternative world. The projectively identified portion of the self then lives on in the ghostline world as its own character. Adrienne, for example, projected a sadistic relation to her father on to her female boss who then became a figure in her imaginary world. The boss had lost her own traits, including her looks and most recognizable features, but certain scraps of clothes and actions signified this figure as, in fact, the boss. Although the actual person of the boss continued to be a perplexing irritant to Adrienne, the real person seemed an irrelevance, except as a sponsor of its transformed double.

The analyst is likely to find himself in an interesting situation with such a patient. In some situations the patient's unrelation to the analyst is such that the analysand preserves an effective false self, perhaps cheerfully bringing details from life into narrative representation, and keeping the imaginary world very split off. My experience with Adrienne, however, suggests that eventually the patient experiences unknown (i.e., unconscious) need for the analyst, which intensifies that order of projective identification described above. That is, the patient struggles to de-incarnate the analyst, to spirit his idiom into a controlled inner psychic space. The patient accomplishes this by incredibly fast projective identifications, reading elements of the self into and beyond the analyst, such as taking an element of an interpretation and lodging an aspect of the self in it. This is then pushed beyond the psyche–soma of the analyst, spirited off into the other space, for transformation into the ghosts of that world. This may give the analysand the appearance of being a keen observer of the analyst, and of having acute perception, but I think this may be misleading, as the patient perceives only part of the other in order to use the part for containment of the projected parts of the self.

An analytical session, then, can have the quality of a reversed seance. The spirit of another is not brought into the room, it is taken out of the analyst–other, and this process has something of the feel of a seance. On many occasions with Adrienne, whom I found likeable and fascinating, I was really quite lost. She would describe states of mind, report events from her day, tell me about her past, in a manner – I can now see – that was her preparation for my 'ghostification'. She would 'feed' me details that sometimes represented parts of herself, such that my interpretation defined me as a spirit, as that ghost whom she cultivated, nourished, and lived with in the long hours of daydreaming. I became aware of my double.

To some extent, of course, this is an exaggeration of what most patients do. Most analysands transform us into a subjective object and possess us within themselves as their own object. But there is an existential interplay between this internal possession and the actual other, an interplay that is effected by instinctual urges, emotional states, idiom evolutions, and self experiences. The patient is present, and we are used in the here and now to process the dynamic articulations of the transference. This is true whether the patient is neurotic, borderline, or even in some respects, psychotic. The particular schizoid patient I describe is not present, but projectively identifies through and beyond the analyst to a collected and secluded alternative space where the subject chooses to live as an alternative to interpersonal life.

Life Against Death

I think the most difficult period in the transference, for such a person, is when they find, through need and experience, that the analyst is alive. It is this aliveness which is painfully troubling as the ghost of the analyst makes sense only in relation to the death of an object. At first, this death, or the putting to death of the object, takes place as an assumed act in the transference. As the analyst analyses this process, however, he finds himself in the midst of an intense other-worldly refusal by the patient, almost a haunting cry of rejection: 'Don't you dare try to bring me back into life!' It is at this point that the multiple deaths of self states come painfully into cognition, as the patient no longer finds relating to the ghosts as capable of processing this aspect of the analysis.

Adrienne and Mary struggled against my life in each session. They forcefully talked about, and sometimes from, the alternate world. They pushed the characters from this world on to the analytic stage, aiming to crowd me out. In each case, as the continuously living object, I became the focus of intense hate and revenge. I was withdrawn from. I was untalked to. I was to be existentially forced into a non-existence, but interestingly, it was the instinctual need, manifested at times in erotic states in the here and now thinking of me, that profoundly disturbed the effective annihilation of me as a living object. Indeed, one can say that it was my life that made it possible for love to emerge and for instinctual urges to emerge and claim their destiny in the sessions.

From intensive counter-cathexis of the analytic object (in the interest of energizing the ghost world), to increasingly aggressive encounter with the analyst: from anti-libidinal dis-incarnation of the life of the analyst to incrementally instinctual urges in the transference, this person re-discovers the transitional object through a begrudging use of the analyst who cannot be got rid of. His ability to survive, his presence and aliveness, resuscitate in the patient archaic experiences of the intermediate area of experiencing. This is not the alternate world. The analyst is not to be transformed into a double to live in the domain of alternate selves in the ghostland. The route to this person's object relating will, then, emerge from aggression and encounter, through a form of 'loving hate' (Bollas, 1987) that permits him to come into the here and now of object relating. This movement is sponsored both by an instinctual re-incarnation of sorts, as the analysand allows instinctual urges to create an object out of the living analyst, and by the destiny drive, the need to articulate one's true self through object usage.

It is the analyst's aliveness, his availability for use-fulness, that elicits the destiny drive and sponsors instinctual and self needs. And it is precisely this use-fulness that the original environment declined to provide this child who had to create and sponsor alternate objects: of the self and the other.

Finally, I do not wish to convey an impression that the alternative world is only a pathology, as, in fact, it serves the right of the subject to preserve and nourish the essence of important self states, potential selves (futures) and significant objects. Indeed, it is quite ordinary for children to create *alter* selves and objects and to need the privacy of the alternative world in order to facilitate the continued existence of such phenomena. Imaginary companions, story book heroes, fairy tale figures, no doubt all contain elements of selves and others particular to the child.

Indeed, I think the child who uses objects transitionally may transport the essence of the object into an alternative world, creating a double of the object, that allows for the actual object to be vigorously owned, authorized from deep within the child's psyche. But, strictly speaking, this is not then an alternative object but the psychic representation of a transitional object. The inner object is linked up with the actual phenomenon, whereas the alternative object is just that: *alter* to the actual. This alterity does, of course, serve an important function for the child who creates passionately present internal objects whom he looks after and imagines each day. To my mind, this is a feature of the conservative process (Bollas, 1987), the inner holding of a state of being, in order that such a state may be given time for mental processing. The child's creation of an imaginary self may be the creation of a conservative object, an inner object that conserves a self state. Children have experiences that are beyond comprehension which they store for eventual knowing (Bollas, 1987). At the moment of its conservation such a self state would constitute an element of the unthought known, of something which is known but beyond thought at that time. By 'sending' a state of being or self into the alternative world where it is transformed into an other who is then internally sustained, the child gives himself time to process his experiences, time that is achieved in this inner space, far removed from the actual world.

We can properly speak, in my view, of a ghostline personality only when the child or adult utilizes the alternative world to conserve the self (and its objects) with little aim of accomplishing an inner thinking of the unthought known as a transition to bringing true self back into negotiation with the actual world. To reaffirm the qualitative differences of the ghostline personality I shall list the significant features.

1. Due to a failure of potential space to emerge between self and other the subject cannot 'live' in the intermediate area of experiencing.

2. The child experiences this as a death of:
   a. a part of the true self or
   b. a potential true self state (future) or
   c. the transitional object.

3. The essence of that which dies is rapidly transferred to a deep inner area of the self.

4. This inner area energizes an alternative world which is for the conservation of self states that are foreclosed for one reason or another.

5. If the subject cannot work through the self state for eventual re-submission to the environment (via play and symbolic representation), the alternative world becomes a kind of incarcerating womb.

6. Self states and object representations subsequently referred to the alternative world bear the affects of a type of death, and whatever form they take in the alternative world, they feel like ghosts – spirits of the departed.

7. The 'ghosts' bear the sense of the dis-incarnation of the psychosomatic self, which is another way of saying they represent true self states dying as they touch the object.

8. The subject then nourishes these spiritual presences, and feels as if he contains many important beings. This is a schizoid phenomenon which can, under certain circumstances, move to a paranoid schizophrenia.

9. Even though these ghosts are kept in a special area of the subject, with no intention to matriculate them into life, they

are part of the conservative process and have the potential for re-incarnation.

10.   I suggest this happens in the transference as the patient experiences the aliveness of the analyst who becomes a transitional object through loving hate.

11.   Alternative objects then transform to true self states and objectified objects through transitional object usage in the transference. The objectified object (the mental representation of an aspect of the mother or father) is then available for its status as an ordinary internal object and can be repressed, or historicized as the memory of the object's integrity.

The transitional object is the infant's first not–me possession. It is loved and hated passionately, because its difference is informed by the subject's use of it.

The alternative object can be considered the infant's first not–other object. It is selected because it is different from the self and the other. The use of alternative objects (actual or mental) to split off the true self – in an imaginary space or in intellectual life – is normal. Each person develops a use of alternative objects that house self and other experience that for one reason or another the subject does not bring into life.

Initially then, the alternative object is difficult to differentiate from the transitional object as both signify difference, but the emphasis is different: the transitional object is not me, the alternative object is not other. The transitional object signifies a creative use of the real, so the not–me object is, ironically, an expression of the me. The alternative object is to be used in fantasizing; it is an object in the imaginary, and is *alter* to the real world.

The child using a transitional object is passionately possessive of it. There is no such passion in the child's use of alternative objects. Indeed, while the child usually has only one transitional object at a time, the child who uses alternative objects has many such phenomena cast about in his life, each the vehicle of a mental flight into the alternative world.

How does one distinguish this alternative world from daydreams? Certainly in the beginning I think the daydeam is an alternative act, a splitting off into a private area. The characters of a daydream may indeed have this special presence to them, as with the ghostline personality. Time and cathexis play some role in differentiating the daydream from the ghostline world. A daydream can be a very nourishing and useful entry into an alternative world to gather together imaginary experiences as a means of thinking something known but not yet thought, or of planning some action. The daydreamer, then, surrenders to this process, and re-enters fully wakeful, living with an addition. But if this crossover into daydreaming is a consistent alternative to creative wakeful life, then its characters will reflect the deaths of self states and potential others. These deaths change the ambience of the alternative world, and the daydreamer must now exert a wilful control over its contents to prevent a catastrophe. Therein the alternative world loses that symbolic process akin to the dream. It becomes a kind of deadening of the dream.

Indeed, the use of alternative objects as I have stressed in this chapter reflects an element of strain in the child's relation to the mother and to cultural objects. When a child spirits off the essence of self states and elements of the other, and transports them to an alternative world where they are transformed into a controlled character, now a feature of an internal theatre, he conserves his self and object world. This conservative process, in which the subject aims to protect endangered parts of the self and experience of the other, differs dramatically from the transitional process where the subject continuously transforms the object in a creative manner.

The generative potential of this process should be clear. Although these conserved states, spirits of self and other, are not creatively elaborated, they do have a potential both for re-externalization to a transitional space and for transitional object use. So although the alternative object is created as the not-other, it stores essential elements of the child's object world which are of potential use to the subject, particularly in the course of a psychoanalysis.

I believe that we have much to learn from this person. Of the patients I have discussed, only Adrienne is a ghostline personality, as the others were either emerging from such a state or were playing with the memory of such a phenomenon. Each of us moves the spirit of a self state or the experience of the other across this inner life, so that each of us has a ghostline and each of us nourishes the spirit of an object (as in mourning), but there are some persons who essentially live in this alternative world, far from the maddening crowds of ordinary internal objects and removed from the pleasures and necessities of interrelating.

7

'Tripping'

W hat does it mean, 'to drop acid'? It brings to mind a casual fall. The subject waits for the chemical to act, anticipating the jolt of its visitation. At the moment of the fall, the drug takes him out of himself, away on 'trips', as he voyages through hallucinated landscapes. The content of a trip is unpredictable. Some are good, some are bad. Like a mood that sweeps over the subject this sudden paroxysm of the psyche casts the tripper into a new frontier. This use of the psyche makes for an interesting relation to the hallucinated contents; it is an exploitative knowledge, the tripper an adventurer who plunders an area of the mind to 'spot' hallucinates. But of course sighting does not equal knowing, even though there is a kind of perverse intrapsychic voyeurism in the user who boasts of his trips. To the psychoanalyst who considers himself an appointed visitor to the fields of the unconscious the tripper's arrogant assertions of actual knowledge can grate on the nerves. In the psychoanalytical treatment of a user it is almost inevitable for the patient to challenge the analyst's sense of privilege in sighting the use.

But the dropping of acid, this casual, almost serene moment, bears as little relationship to the violent outcome as the atom bomb dropping from the plane's bay is linked to Hiroshima. Such utter simplicity – 'Just drop it, easily done, you see' – becomes grotesque in the light of the horror to follow. Of course, the acid dropper would object to this metaphor. After all, this is a drop that also pleases, it 'sends' the tripper to extraordinary places. If so, then these micro-Hiroshimas annihilate the subject who is sent into a post-explosive landscape of deceptive pleasures. Is it not possible that among the victims of Hiroshima, in that first burst of light, a few hallucinated its opposite and saw a resplendent flash of the miraculous?

Violating the Subjective

Hallucinating from ingestion of a drug is an act of violence against one's subjectivity. It differs from ordinary vivid psychic phenomena, such as dreams, because the ego is not working on that psychic evolution that is its tradition in making a dream. This involves a complex circuiting of co-ordinating affects, moods, day residue, evoked memories, and instinctual drives to fashion them into a drama which brings the potential dreamer to the dream space for participation.

One of the ego's tasks is to integrate and synthesize at any moment a digestible sample of the infinite possible combinations of psychic elements and lived experience. The co-ordinating task is made realizable because each person has a self, a limiting set of intrapsychic perspectives, and ego integration will ultimately be bound by the knowledge and tasks of this self.

The sudden transformation precipitated by a drug will not have been the ego's work, although ego will process this violence. The action of the drug is chemical, and it usurps the ego's work to sustain the psyche. At any one moment, in a dream, or in a fantasy, the subject imagines events and people, and through such self and object representation, an internal world is sustained which is the stuff of psyche. Ego work makes psychic life possible, at least as a material content that is available for reflection (as in dream reporting, or considering the daydream) and further elaboration (as in the next dream, or the subsequent daydream). If we cannot speak of a relation between ego and psyche we can say that there is a connection between the two, and though ego will always exist as long as the brain is alive, psyche is dependent on ego to exist.

The drug user's potion breaks the ordinary link between ego and psyche. The ingestion of a chemical usurps the ego's work and places the subject in a more immediate and unmediated view of the pathways of instinct and percept. We may ask, 'Why would anyone want to do this to himself?', but it may be timely to wonder, 'Who is doing this, to whom, and about what?' – a question derived from Paula Heimann's (1956) theory of the transference as the enactment of an object relation. On the basis of her theory, it is not possible to assume that anyone ever acts alone. It is within keeping of her perspective to wonder whether such ingestion is an act of identification by a drug user, who may re-create some essential element of a former feeding situation, one that overwhelmed the ego.

I am struck by a common experiential factor. In all those addicts I have seen or whose treatment I have supervised, the mother and father appear psychically removed from their children. The reasons for this removal vary, of course, although they seem to share an aspect of what I term the normotic element: an aversion to subjectivity and a preference for making oneself into a thing–object, to sit alongside the material object worlds as a companion of sorts. Such parents cannot cathect the child who is not to be part of the parents' psychic elaboration and so the child receives impaired mirroring from the mother or the father.

In the case of the drug user, I think we can speak of a person who, when a child, was deeply lonely and isolated. Perhaps this is the child whose parents worked, came home for a quiet dinner, exiled the children to bed, and watched television. Or this was the child whose mother was an alcoholic and who was boozy and boring. These are the more typical situations, but it is equally possible (though less common, I think) for a drug user to come from a family whose parents were stimulating and responsive. Some of the acting-out patients Winnicott writes about are people who come from upper middle class homes where the parents are active and intellectually alive, but where the child feels his intellectual life is false and he lives at a cost to his own sense of inner reality.

Alternately, some drug addicts may have sided with a death instinct and have withdrawn from the parents, nullifying parental ability. It is possible to see this occur in small doses when children sulk, deadening themselves as an attack on the parent. A child may never forgive a parent, say, for introducing a rival. Sibling hate may be sufficient cause for a child to remove himself from parenting and to impose a deadening isolation on himself. In later life the person may withdraw from conflicts, particularly those that excite envy and sibling hate. Such destructiveness is partly sustained by a sense of power, as this person manages to defeat the loving efforts of those close to him who are trying to nurture him into creativity. I am sure this must be true of some adolescents, for example, who use drugs in order to elicit a parental concern (love) in order to destroy it. This solicitation and destruction of love is part of the death instinct, and the processes invoked have been cogently argued by Herbert Rosenfeld (1987), who claims that the destructive narcissist, for example, idealizes the destructive side of his personality because it makes him feel powerful. 'When destructive narcissism of this kind is a feature of a patient's character structure, libidinal (that is to say, loving, caring, interdependent) object relationships and any wish on the part of the self to experience the need for an object and to depend on it are devalued, attacked, and destroyed with pleasure' (p. 22).

Intrapsychic Exhibitionism

Whether a person recreates a parent's removal or his own inner psychic removal, one of the features of the user's intrapsychic states is his distance from the contents of the psyche. In this respect he reminds one of the pervert's 'distance' from the emotional reality of psychic content, which the pervert organizes into a ritual. The user and the pervert watch the happenings of mind and instead of insight, there is an intrapsychic exhibitionism.

Such a split between seeing and feeling constitutes a compromise formation between a surrender to a painful experience of psychic reality and a total remove where no contact is made with the inner world. This compromise, again one that reminds us of the pervert, establishes excitement as a prevailing feeling, encompassing anxiety and distance. As he awaits his first hallucination, the user is the expectant voyeur and later, when he narrates tales of discovery, he will do so in an excited state.

I believe this split occurs because the user tries to form a kind of self–other relation, by taking the mother's and father's place in relation to the child's imaginative elaboration of instinctual life. By feeding himself, he develops and manages a situation that originated with the mother and his self-feeding is perhaps not unlike the infant's feed, in that it is both exhilarating and frightening – as if, in the drug, the user has found an object that exemplifies the ambivalent experience of feeding at the mother's breast. Again, however, the user now controls the process. Is it possible that his relation to the drug, as both the stimulus and the imagined container of hallucinations, approximates this person's course of projections in relation to the mother? Is it possible that as such a child experiences his imaginative life as unusually sponsored (or curtailed) by the mother's actions, that he imagines his phantasy life to be somehow 'in' her? This would be consistent with one view – that the mother and father have not mirrored the infant and child back to himself; they have not reflected him, nor have they elaborated his gestures and communications, enabling him to feel understood and enhanced by object relating. Instead, the child will associate imagining with the comings and goings of the mother and father, as if it happens in relation to their presence or absence. One of the effects of this phantasy is that the child projects his psychic life into the object, associating its messages with an external object. In this sense, then, the user's relation to the drug, as the imagined container of psychic phenomena, continues the child's projection of psychic life into the mother, whose person and presence is associated with imagining.

It has been a feature of my argument on the nature of the normotic parent to state that they do not enjoy the subjective; they do not like the play of imagination. So the child of normotic parents will not feel that his imaginative life is inside a container that flourishes in the process of using such imaginative products; instead, projection into the container equals extinction. I consider this phantasy to be inextricable from the user's object relations: projection is associated with the extinction of life, and therefore there is always a sense of death about.

But a user could feel that his life is 'in' the object, if, as a child, he was inordinately preoccupied with destructive attacks on the mother and father. When this is true the child (and later adolescent) mutilates the parental mirror, so that he extracts a distorted view of himself, often with the aim of selecting a parental comment which seems to support his sense of persecution. When this form of hate prevails, the child is inevitably incarcerated in his internal object world, as all the other parts of himself (in particular the loving feelings) are bound inside hateful and hated object representatives. The sight of the actual parent can inspire an immediate deadening hate, and the adolescent may feel a need to break out of this persecutory world into a universe of lovely and thrilling alternatives.

The Sense of Death

The sense of death is, of course, a feature of that risk that is also an essential part of the drug user's relation to drugs. He knows, as do we, that drugs kill. This is not an unfortunate hazard or an incidental feature of the user's life. The possibility of death is an essential part of what the user is gambling on. It is part of his reorganization of a childhood when projection meant extinction and the death of the self.

As the tripper contemplates the paper that is soaked in acid, or as he holds a pill in his hand, he holds an object that in itself indicates nothing of what it contains or will sponsor. It is a totally banal object. In that sense it is an appropriate symbolic representative of the mother or the father. There it is, an object with no indication of what it contains, just as the mother and father bear no trace of having reared this child.

When he puts the banal object into his mouth and waits for the trip to take him, he may also indicate something of the history of experiencing the arrivals of mother and father. In some cases, the childhood is lived in prolonged loneliness, with little parental facilitation of the child's idiom. This may be due to a true parental failure or to the child's destructive attacks on the parent. As such, the person is unpractised in ordinary introspection or in creative elaboration of psychic life. An event such as a troubling dream, for example, will have a curious status in this child's life. On the one hand vivid and suggestive of meaning, it will have to exist in a kind of vacuum, unrelated to the child's environment, unelaborated on through imaginative play or representation to the parents for processing. The same will be true of daydreams, which, though intense, will not be elaborated and will be cut off and isolated from life itself. The hallucination arrives out of banal existence like an explosion, giving an overwhelming intensity to subjective life. The same can be said of this child's ordinary experience of subjective states which seem to arise out of lonesome emptiness. The question is,

'What can the user or child do with such overwhelming arrivals of the subjective?' As a child, he cannot or will not take the dream, the phantasy, or the potential play creation to the mother or father. How does the ego cope with this authority of the psyche, an intense moment that cannot find its way to transformation?

I believe the child projects it into the mother and father where it is extinguished. Subjective life is associated with anti-parental activity, and it is rather quickly placed into the mother for her riddance of it. It is more pertinent to say that the child projects the process of dream and phantasy into the mother whose container function is one of extinguishing psychic life and deadening it to allow the child to be a thing–object living in harmony with other thing–objects; or he projects the extinguished idea into the helpful mother, insisting that she bear his deadness. It can be seen, then, that the user's ingestion of the banal is a reversal of this procedure, as he takes back into himself the process of psychic life and the mother's container function: the elements of extinction and death. Ordinarily these elements will constitute the aftermath of the hallucinations proper as the user feels extinguished and deadened, a kind of macabre representation of the containing process: from psychic life to psycho-somatic extinction. Sometimes the user overdoses and death will claim him.

No child, however, totally accepts a normotic disposition to his own private requirements. If it is true that his psychic life cannot find elaboration and therefore transformation through the mother's and father's care, then I think such a child will store untransformed states of being and self for a potential transformation in the future. I have described such a procedure as a conservative process, in that the child conserves an experience relatively unchanged and untransformed in the hope that some day it can be lived out in the presence of a more transforming object (such as a friend, partner, or analyst). Unfortunately, for the user there has been a massive over-utilization of this conservative process, fating this person to an overstorage of undigested, painful experiences.

Repeated use of hallucinogenic drugs establishes a violent subjectivity in which the bizarre happenings of the internal world violate the subject's capacity to sustain a core self. In the course of analysing an adolescent who had used drugs repeatedly, it was clear that drug-taking 'sent' him to a familiar place, which clearly was 'to' the psychotic part of his personality. After a year of analysis, during an intensely florid psychosis, he remembered previous psychotic attacks during his early childhood. His panic, tearfulness, and rage during this period of the analysis was moving testimony to the several psychotic breakdowns he endured as a child. All of the memories recovered were terrors associated with parental failure to ensure his safety. Whether these events really happened or whether he dreamed them up is hardly the issue here. Indeed, a dream invention may more tellingly describe the child's fears of the world than actual memories of frightening incidents.

By dropping acid at least once a day for four years, this patient gained a pseudo-mastery over the psychotic parts of his personality, as he determined the moment of onset. Indeed, during a non-drug-inspired psychotic period (lasting two months) he desperately searched his memory to recall what he might have eaten that would have caused the attack. After the acid trip, the patient would be 'dead' for many hours, a death that, as I have suggested, is an intrinsic part of the acid trip. In a larger sense we could term this the death of self that follows violent subjectivity.

A Search for Transformation

At some point a question arises: 'Who or what can possibly serve as a transformational object for such a person?' It is most unfortunate indeed that the drug appears to do just this. The power of the drug to push this passive and deadened person through the illusion of transformation is so convincing that the user feels he has found a transformational object that is capable of dealing with massive overconservation of being and self states. I think it is understandable that the user should feel this way. And we can see the problem that the therapist or analyst has in enabling this person to accept that ordinary transformational object that the analyst is, and to discover in the ordinary work of analysis – in clarifications, interpretations, and silences – the value of object relating.

Further, this object is a completely external one. Psychic life is in the pill or the piece of paper. In this sense, the user indicates another reversal. The products of imaginative life usually come through the unconscious, through the preconscious to consciousness to use Freud's model, or, through a state of quiet which is receptive to the thinking of the as yet unthought, a receptiveness that sponsors the evocation of the unthought known and facilitates generative musing on that which is brought into consciousness. This is an exceedingly complex intrapsychic process, and although of course elements of this procedure are to be found in the tripper, his aim is to procure thoughts only through the object. This drug, which is taken in the mouth, will be excreted some hours later. It is the sole sponsor of subjectivity. Its power and distinctiveness in his life is determined by its otherness and strangeness. The user does not want to maintain contact with his inner world. Or, to put it differently, he wants to keep his psychic life in the pill. Imagination is to come out of deadness, not out of receptiveness. Phantasy is to emerge from a necrophilic excitement in relation to the deadened self: 'Let's see what it does to me now!' There is no musing, no evoking.

The user does not transform the hallucination into insight and trips are not introspective experiences, even though the subject appears to have an abundance of material for reflection. It is crucial to the tripper's relation to his psyche that it is 'in' the pill or the paper, that psychic life visits the user in a flash, and that equally it wears off and moves toward somatic inertness. But what of the intellectual merits of continuous drug trips? Would it be true to say that this person's journey into uncharted regions of enforced psychosis are of no worth? Certainly I don't think we can claim that drugs only constitute cheap thrills, and later in this chapter I will discuss some of the truly frightening features of the intellectual journey that is part of this world. But insightfulness is not one of the outcomes of such continuous searches into hallucinatory consciousness. Indeed, the tripper must keep the agencies of insight external to himself, notably in the pill or the paper which over time is associated with the containment of the psychic content that it sponsors. The paper-thin sample of acid is strikingly like a micro-chip which stores another world.

The drug user, however, is capable of a kind of extrospection, by which I mean a reversal of the process of introspection: an intense looking into the other. So users can congregate in groups, narrate their hallucinations, and subject one another to rather complex and intricate analyses of hallucinations. But the destruction of insight is carried forward in its projection so that the extrospection is not truly insightful.

Endopsychic Perceptions

I t seems to me highly likely that continued hallucinations enable the user to gain heightened endopsychic perception. It must be the case that some of the hallucinations represent psychic structure itself, so that some of the contents are representations of the projector, the machinery of the mind, rather than its content. Indeed, there is probably a kind of formal neurological regression, with more primitive parts of the brain being active in hallucinatory and allied experiences, possibly giving way to endopsychic representations. As such, the user does see into the depths of his creation, and some of his preoccupations (often depicted in his artwork) will reflect this formal regression. In that sense the user has been somewhere both strange and familiar, and he has climbed inside himself in ways that few of us are ever likely to do, except perhaps, in the seconds before our death.

If it is true that psyche evolves from a true self (an inherited core), and is elaborated and altered through negotiation with the mother's and father's rules for being and relating, then the user's movement, back to the origins of mental functioning, back to the transfer from the primitive instinctive parts of the brain to the developed parts, becomes an ironic fixation indeed. It is as if he adamantly returns to the transitional area which he could never use – the transition from primitive instinctive functioner to human being. For so much of what it means for us to be human has to do with communicating and representing ourselves through language, an accomplishment never truly achieved by the user, except at the level of false self.

The use of drugs, then, permits the tripper to return to a transitional area which he failed to utilize, the transition from instinctive creature to human being. In using the drugs to activate more primitive parts of the brain, he conjures up memories of pre-human experiences, before he sensed his idiom, his subjective status, his significance to the other.

Issues of Treatment

What are the tasks unique to the treatment of a user? Because one of the user's most consistent means of self-protection is not to know, specifically to destroy the mind's containing function by severing links between thoughts, one of the analyst's most difficult tasks is to analyse what the tripper is doing within the here and now.

One day a patient came to his session early. I had some visitors, and when there was a knock at the door I was surprised to see my patient there. He looked confused, and I sensed his forlornness. I said that I was sorry but he must have had his hour wrong and reminded him of his afternoon schedule. Some five hours later, he entered the room in a curiously tranquil state and sat down. Slowly and captivatingly he removed his watch from his wrist and stared at it. He put it to his ear. He then asked me if I had a pen. At that moment I was unable to understand the nature of his question – that is, to link his request with what he was going – and he explained that he needed a pen to set his watch right. It was one of those watches that required one to push a pen or narrow object into a small opening to set the hour, minute, date, and so forth. He was unable to do this even though he is an exceptionally intelligent and able person. This went on for some minutes; and when he said that the minute indicator was flashing, I told him to push the pen again to get the hour, which is what he wanted to achieve. Eventually we got his watch working, but I realized that I had given him the wrong date. I had said it was the 7th when in fact it was the 6th. So we had to reset the watch. I wish I could say that immediately he became absorbed with his watch I thought to myself that, of course, this was an elaboration of the confusion over time; but the fact is that I became absorbed in his preoccupation, which had a very compelling quality to it, a wordless, thoughtless quality. Everything seemed to be in slow motion. On reflection we can see that the patient was trying to get me to accept responsibility for time confusion, and indeed I did accept it unconsciously as I obliged by giving him the wrong date, for which I apologized. Depending on one's analytic persuasion, we could say that in this respect I was empathically in tune with him or that I was the victim of his projective identification. My interpretation to him was, 'Well, we are trying to put the watch right, but I muck you up, as you felt I did this morning when you came to our room and I was not able to see you'. He replied, 'Who were those people?'

I use this ordinary moment and interpretation to indicate how a simple interpretation of the meaning of an act is a vital element in the user's psychic development; an ordinary act of clarification and interpretation is essential, not so much to build up a store of knowledge, but to activate and establish mental processes, particularly linking and reflective functions. In other words, I utilized the following mental processes: perception, memory, reflection, linkage between two phenomena, imaginative elaboration.

As the analyst works to establish and restore the damaged parts of the user's mind, he can become more important to the patient as an ordinary transformational object. If the analysand comes across a difficulty in life (say with a girlfriend) and needs to discuss it with the analyst, then the analyst's thoughtfulness is in itself helpful. From the perspective of Bion, this would be equivalent to the analyst's establishment of his function as a container, and the patient would increasingly use this container to process his psychic content.

Because of his deadness and extreme suspicion, the tripper often cannot associate to the events of his life. It is not good, either, for the analyst to go fishing, by asking a hundred questions, leading him through an interrogative world. Instead, I think the analyst may need to become the associative factor in the session, truly reflecting on the patient's material by saying, 'What you have said brings to my mind …', or 'That reminds me of a previous session'. I have found unintrusive free association of true value to such patients who come to understand in the here and the now of the analyst's mental functioning what is meant by free association, even if this phrase is never used by the analyst. The patient comes to understand what is meant when he is asked to say what comes to his mind. I also think that the selective disclosure of certain details from one's life helps the tripper to feel that he is part of a collectively human experience, rather than a specimen of the freakish. Such persons really do lose their sense of perspective after a long period of drug abuse. They truly do not know what is freakish and what is human. Indeed they can develop a persecuting superego that adjudges all of their phantasies and dreams as para-criminal acts which must be kept under lock and key.

One day I knew that my patient with the watch was struggling to become cognizant of his sexual feelings about a female patient. He was intensely persecuted by his drives and totally suspicious of me. I was a cop. At such a moment he would not have been helped, in my view, had I analysed his fear of me as simply due to his projection of a persecuting part of his mind that attacked him for ordinary sexual feelings. I think such a comment would have helped a bit, but unfortunately not enough, and as such, with this kind of person, it would have been wrong. Users have lived so long in the false self, developing a part self to partly process social relations, that I think they are experts at colluding with part acts. The analytic interpretation above would, in my view, have felt to this patient like my device for extracting his fantasies. Instead, I chose to say, 'Ah, Ladies. Ladies. Ladies! What would we do without them!' which broke the ice, and he laughed. I then said, 'You know when I was your age there was a beautiful girl, absolutely stunning, who used to sit in my English class. I couldn't think. I'd take one look at her, and I was gone. She had me, totally. I died in every class!' He then proceeded for some twenty minutes non-stop to tell me that he too was captured by a girl by whom he felt persecuted, and so on. My disclosure, which was true of my life, is true of all our lives. Each of us has fallen into a kind of erotic stupor in adolescence which shuts down the brain. And inside this experience is the idea of being captured, of being frustrated, of feeling silly, and so forth – ideas that I knew this patient was trying to process. Perhaps I could have found a way of enabling this patient to discuss such ideas without disclosing such an episode from my own life, but in subsequent months when my patient reviewed the analysis with me, the one feature he singled out that he thought had helped him, from a technical point of view, was my self-disclosure.

The analyst's associations inspire in a drug user an interest in ordinary subjective life. An object (the analyst) is found to be interesting. The user listens intently, feels an affinity with the analyst's affects, and associates to the analyst's contents. Gradually the patient develops a working belief in human relating. Disabling the mind (the patient's or the analyst's) to nullify inner experience and object relations lessens as the patient finds relief and pleasure in the interplay of subjectivities to be found in the clinical situation.

Through a combination of intensive confrontation of the patient's destructive mental processes and the use of one's own subjectivity as a source of 'play' the analyst can create a viable transitional space for the user whose Faustian partnership with drugs has been to see everything and to know nothing.

8

The Anti-Narcissist

The ongoing non-idealized but loving cathexis of one's self is an essential feature of ordinary narcissism. If one of the salient features of mature love is a true knowledge of the loved object, a knowing that is informed by a sense of the many aspects of the other, then mature love would be a knowing that is informed by the realities of all parts of this self. Most individuals are endowed with a positive narcissism. We have an informed affection for ourselves so that the problematic parts of the self are confronted in a responsible and forgiving way rather than being subjected to a merciless tirade. And this love we have for ourselves is a continuous source of inner nourishment.

It is striking, therefore, when we meet someone who does not possess positive narcissism, but indeed who cultivates a negative narcissism. Certainly there is an intense masochistic feature to this act, as Green has explored. (For a compelling discussion of the divergent aims of what he terms *narcissisme de vie* and *narcisissme de mort* one should consult Green's fascinating exploration of creative and destructive narcissism (Green, 1987).)

The anti-narcissist opposes his own destiny. As he forecloses his true self, refusing to use objects to articulate his idiom, he is of special interest to me. For as he negates his destiny, this anti-elaborative person 'stews in his own juice' and adamantly refuses to nurture himself. He may come to an analyst precisely in order to defeat the aims of analysis. To capture the nature of this patient's misuse of the analytic object I shall provide two brief vignettes.

Giovanni

Giovanni was an Italian composer who was referred to me by a colleague. I was told that he was exceptionally talented and loved by many people. Clearly the referrer thought he was something of a gift, and I could see why he thought this. Apparently a wonderfully whimsical person, he came to his first session in clothing which had been specially made for him, and his choice of colours was in exceptionally good taste.

If his account of his life was melancholically conveyed, it was not out of place. His parents had been poor. His father was an alcoholic and something of a neighbourhood desperado. He would crawl into bedrooms that contained one or another of his local sweethearts, and he seemed to have started this as a boy and practised it until his death some five years before Giovanni came to analysis. Giovanni's mother was first called an 'angel', although when he said this the word seemed to stick in his throat. Once he said, 'I must confess. My mother adored *me*. I was a *treasure*.' He emphasized certain words with such force it virtually sunk him to the bottom of some inner sea. Each time he spoke of her love of him he stressed himself as her object in such a way as to convey his lack of personal authorship of his own existence: 'I was her *darling*', 'She thought I could do no *wrong*'.

As time passed, I was puzzled by Giovanni's profound refusal to use analysis. What I initially saw as a colourful nature to his character was, I discovered, the fish to bait the hook. I had been taken in by his apparently promising personality. For a moment I had a vision of his future, which I cathected in a thoughtful manner.

Indeed this was his unconscious strategy in the transference. As in all his relations in life, he seduced people into investing him as a future object. I had looked forward to an interesting and rewarding analytic experience. Others who knew him would, no doubt, have looked forward to some future with him. But my sense of a mutual destiny, involving reciprocal object use, was the very factor Giovanni evoked in me in order to destroy it.

I cannot detail the analysis of him, and, instead, I shall focus on an error in my own work with him. Giovanni talked at length about the relation to his father, who seemed to me to be not only the rival for the mother but his own object of love. After some six months of analysis

Giovanni lost his job, and I took this to be a genuine loss. It was a time of comprehensive economic decline in England (many people were losing their jobs), and I said that he could continue at a reduced fee until he was re-employed. This we did for nearly a year. This misplaced generosity on my part only made Giovanni's negativity, particularly his self-loathing worse. At the end of this year he moved abroad with his girlfriend who had found employment.

I erred by providing him with analysis at a low fee, thereby personifying the beneficent mother, whose love is so boundless that it overrides considerations of reality (his and mine). It colluded with that part of him that felt exceedingly special to the mother, but in a way that was highly dissociated from reality. My continuation of his analysis became increasingly unrealistic.

How had this happened? I failed to see that he preoccupied himself with his father in our sessions partly in order to avoid considering the mother. I was taken in by this because he spoke to me in 'man talk': commenting on football games, telling me about a beautiful woman he had just seen on the street, describing his relations to male and female colleagues in a certain 'tough' way. The relation to his mother, and the mother's relation to him, was less a focus on our parts, although, as I suggested, we acted it out through his unemployment (regression to infancy) and my provision of analysis at a low cost (maternal care).

After the unplanned termination of Giovanni's analysis, I would often reflect on it and wonder where I had gone wrong and what I would do differently. One element, which I consider now, is his destruction of my investment in him. He knew that my provision of analysis at a low fee was due to my belief that analysis could be of use to him, and it was for precisely this reason that he destroyed it. I had mistakenly assumed that Giovanni's destruction of analysis was due to the intensity of unconscious guilt over my provision, and it was to this guilt and what I assumed to be his anger toward me that I directed many of my comments.

I was convinced at the time that this was the proper emphasis. Giovanni's self-recrimination increased: 'Oh you shouldn't waste your time on me! I'm such a pile of shit!' Sessions were not exclusively preoccupied with such berations, but after reporting a dream, or memory, or a detail from his life, which I would interpret, he would inevitably say: 'God, what a clever comment. You are *so* brilliant. And I'm not worth such thinking. Poor me. I'm such a little shit!' I did regularly congratulate him at such a moment for shitting on me, yet appearing innocent of any destruction. I also commented on his fury that something of interest could come from me, and he could not bear this. Interpretation in the area of his envy and his attempt to devalue me by castigating himself were often the focus of my comments.

Unfortunately, it was not until some three years later that I understood what I had not grasped in Giovanni's analysis. This occurred when James, a Lancashire sculptor, came to analysis.

James

Like Giovanni, James was a promising patient. I looked forward to working with him. And like Giovanni, he seized up and proceeded to revile himself. The father was also the frequent object of focus, but with James it was clearer to me how this focus was a wish for the father to be present as an object of and for conflict, rather than the removed parent he had in fact been.

James was less self-destructive than Giovanni and more willing to tell me about his mother than to act it out. His mother was someone who had adored him. He could do no wrong. He was a talented painter as a boy, and his mother arranged for him to have art exhibitions in small, tourist villages in the Midlands. As James's talent was exceptional, he received considerable regional attention, and by his adolescence he was a celebrity. As he began to sculpt, his products were quickly bought up, and his mother's adoration of him seemed quite merited.

Like Giovanni, James collapsed into a profoundly controlling negativity in his analysis. He insisted he was 'psychotic', or 'a pervert', and he presented me with thoughts or sexual fantasies which he insisted were firm evidence of his conviction. As he was neither psychotic nor a pervert, I could not comply with his wish that I see him as such, and he concluded by telling me that I did not take him seriously and that it was his misfortune to have selected an analyst who lacked profundity. He had read psychoanalytic literature that depicted entrenched conflicts between a patient's death instincts and the analyst's unwavering interpretation of such onslaughts. He had expected analysis to be an ennobling enterprise where we would make heroes of one another in trench warfare. At other times he berated me for failure to live up to the Spencerian world of conflict between good and evil that he assumed a 'real' or 'deep' analysis would give.

It is clear to me that he wanted to put me in a certain position: I was at the mercy of a shallow part of my own mind that acted on narcissistically driven love which I used to draw him into a false world of admiration. I loved my love of him. He, in turn, was determined to destroy my good feelings for him, which he intended to do by denigrating my analytic capability. Perhaps he could bring me to my senses. Then I would see that he was a psychotic pervert who needed analytic absolution before he ended his life.

There were some interesting contradictions in his view of himself. First, when I did interpret his destructive actions, he would fly into immediate outrage: 'You are being too critical!' or 'This is just the sort of thing my father might say!' But his father actually had not been critical of him. The father had been distant, and it was the father's removal that James found so troubling.

Second, James was an unconsciously helpful patient. He did report his states of mind even when ironically telling me that he had no intention of doing so: 'Well I'm not going to tell you what I think today, because I want you to suffer and feel that you have failed as an analyst. I'm going to tell you that I feel like committing suicide so that you will have a lousy weekend.' He would also regularly present me with his dreams, report details of his life that were analytically relevant, and he attended all sessions regularly. He did not act out, although much of what he said suggested he was always on the verge of doing so.

Neither Giovanni nor James was a burden to me. I did not experience them as demanding. In spite of their searing and acrid denunciations of themselves, and disparaging views of me, there was a generative 'as if' quality to it. Each of them had an acute sense of the analytic theatre and used this space to genuinely portray their inner world.

It was after some fifteen months with James's analysis that I began to realize what I had not seen before. It became clear to me that he experienced his mother's love of him as a rejection! As if the mother said to the infant: 'James, you don't need me. You have and are everything. Feed upon yourself, my love.' In other words, he experienced the mother as exploiting his true self to fob him off: 'Feed off your own wonderful self rather than upon me'. Thus his personal idiom was not articulated or elaborated through his own use of the mother as an object. Instead he was translated into a small deity whose very artistic production was glorious.

To be sure, James did partly enjoy this idolization. And it was still there when I commented on some part of him that did not inspire worship. Of course he was free, in an act of largesse, to knock himself down, but no one else could criticize him. And he also partly enjoyed his oedipal triumph over the father who tended to leave him to the mother's agency. In the analysis it became clear to me that he was indeed determined not to live according to that inner creativity that is the movement of the true self. Although he was very talented, he had carefully arranged his career so that he could avoid being truly successful. Had this been the extent of his self-limitation we might say that perhaps this was an understandable act on his part, as he experienced success as depersonalization, just as he experienced the mother's idolization as splitting him.

But James's destructive work went further than this. He was a sourpuss who attacked himself all the time. He neglected himself and was often quite ill. He had married a woman who detested sexual life, and who came alive only through acute attacks of hate toward him. In the analysis I found a striking discrepancy between his use of me, which did indeed reflect a true self use of the object, and his self representations which were consistently bad. Over time I brought this to his attention, something which he resisted intensely, because the evidence was based upon the here and now transference and was undeniable. Naturally, he suspected that I was trying to fob him off by projecting an introject of the idolized James into him, but as I analysed his experience of the mother and how he dismantled himself to undo her projections, to spite her, in order to feel self-generated, he gradually understood his predicament and in time gained substantial relief through this work.

Oedipus Complex

What about the father? Both Giovanni and James began their analysis by talking at length about the father. Am I simply ejecting the father from the scene of conflict by focusing on the mother?

Each of these patients was indeed searching for the father in me. I failed Giovanni, because I acted out an unprocessed maternal response and thereby deprived him of his effort to find and process the father. What was he seeking? I think it was conflict. Conflict with the father. As with James, the father was out of the picture, not only because the mother idolized the child but because the child used the mother's idolizations to exclude the father.

We could say that James and Giovanni shared at least one feature in common with Oedipus. They did not have the good fortune to have an oedipus complex. It is striking, I think, that Oedipus did not have that conflict that we associate with his name, because an oedipal scene, in order to become a complex, requires the father's participation. When Laius chose to obey the oracle, and exiled his child, he refused to engage with his son in the oedipal conflict. It is this conflict that he avoided, perhaps because the oracle spoke a split–off voice in Laius, in a paranoid–schizophrenic universe, where conflict was not tolerated. The crossroads was, then, a failed act of integration; there was only collision and death. Had they been engaged in oedipal conflict, had Laius had many prior father–son combats with Oedipus, he would certainly have known his boy and each would have recognized the other at the otherwise fateful crossroads.

What I failed to realize with Giovanni, but did perceive with James, was that each of these people sought me out *in order to have conflict with me*. Each session was a crossroads. And they wanted to drive with great force into this colliding object world, possessed of no insight (no knowledge of who I was) so that I – the father – would assume my responsibility to name the action, to identify myself, and to lead my son into consciousness of our relationship. James presented himself in each session with no apparent memory of a prior session, and no apparent recognition of me as an analyst meeting him for professional reasons. He would report himself frankly, as I have said, but he apparently held on to nothing. This was, as I came to understand, his way of insisting that conflict continue, that he be allowed to fight, and be thoughtless, and insist that I name the scene. The preoccupation with the father was partly a need for those elements of intersubjective life that the father provides. Feeling isolated by maternal idolization, the child seeks the father's generative tough-mindedness, spoiling for a fight that will bring him into an increasingly more real relation to the environment. Eventually I realized that these patients' discussion of the father was a transference request for my paternal capacity to provide combat.

The Fateful Self

As if to punctuate his fury that the early object world refuses his use of the object, the anti-narcissist dismantles his true self movements and constructs a negative false self which he contrives with merciless glee.

By casting himself in a bad light he destroys himself as the mother's object and attacks her thoughtless worship with an equal dose of thoughtless hate. Indeed, James would present his mother with self-denigrating observations, which she would counter with increased doses of praise: 'Oh, don't be silly. A man like you. You are so talented. The world is your oyster.' James would meet this with either a comment or an action which fated him to an unnourishing situation. The most the mother could say was, 'I don't know what to do with you!' as if he were still, even in his worst moments, something which she could still transform into something wonderful if only she knew how to do it.

Insofar as he did not feel the master of his own destiny, James decided to exemplify his status as a master of fate. As the mother's possession, he demonstrated the status of the subject that is removed from his own destiny. Thus he delivered oracular views of his worthlessness which were striking as they seemed so incompatible with his true worth and talent. Even the mother was perplexed by his representations, which she felt to be out of place. She did not know, of course, that it was his unconscious intent that she should experience a situation in which she was witness to a representational assignment that was deeply offensive to the reality of the subject. As she was powerless to get James to change this horrid objectification of himself, so too James had been unable to wean the mother from her paralysing representations of him.

As she had imagined a mutual destiny, driven by his talent and her agency, the mother was to become a frustrated victim of the interventions of fateful self representations, disturbing dislocations of the sense of destiny. James's attack on his mother's futures was devastatingly cruel, and fortunately for her one of the outcomes of his analysis was the emergence and practice of forgiveness as he came to understand why she was the way she was.

The Anti-Narcissist

By dismantling his positive self cathexis the anti-narcissist refuses to be complicitous with the other's love of himself. In his relation to himself as an object (Bollas, 1987) he opposes the mother's adoration by desecrating himself. Although this anti-narcissistic act does embody a covert grandiosity (he will be the grandest failure, the worst monster), it is nonetheless an effective means of unconsciously attacking his destiny. Objects are not used for true self movement but are coralled into a repetitious theatre preoccupied with negative representations.

In a curious way, the anti-narcissist envies his own abilities. He hates his talent, because it is this factor which deprives him of true dependence on the mother. As a gifted painter (as James had been in boyhood), the talent is nominated by the mother as a source of endless nurture. The anti-narcissist looks into the pond and sees a resplendent reflection that is indeed endowed with a wealth of talent. But he sees in this reflection a figure so beyond his true inner state, and apparently endowed as a never-emptied breast of talent, that he feels an intense envy of the implied representation. He does not feel this inner nature, but he sees that if he lives out this talent he will indeed be constantly fed with praise and admiration; or, to be more accurate, that 'it' – the reflection – will be the object of such idolatry.

So when gazing upon his reflection, the anti-naricissist feels enraged by this enviable object and because it deprives him of *a true* relation to the mother, and of the world of give and take, the anti-narcissist casts a stone into the pond to shatter the image.

I wish to stress that the destruction is more an attack on the image (self representations) than upon the true self. The anti-narcissist does not beat himself on the head or pummel his own body. He throws a stone at the representation. And although he does not use the object (specifically the personality elements of the other) to field the true self, the anti-narcissist does employ cultural objects, and does sustain a minimally creative development. I think he does this because he hopes that his situation will be understood, and by conserving the anti-narcissistic posture, he invites the analyst to confront him through the integrating elements of a psychoanalysis.

Negative False Self

Curiously enough, this person constructs a non-compliant false self that hides and sustains a true self. He eventually appears to be anti-social, a malcontent, or a sourpuss, but not in a vicious manner. Like Jaques in *As You Like It* he casts stones in order to invite a challenging conflict. He is a false self in search of a differentiated intellectual aggression that will conflict with the false self, and break it down through sentient intelligence: through analysis. It is the analyst's clinical shrewdness that is sought after, and this factor becomes very important in the patient's struggle to abandon the negative false self.

Gradually he feels understood. Through the complex provision of maternal and paternal elements, the patient feels that the mother and the father are both present in responsible and intelligent ways. They are not there to project grandiose dreams into the patient, puffing up his talents into a dissociative representation. While celebrating his talents, they also meet his requirements as a child (in the analysis, as the child parts of the self), and as this occurs the patient senses that the object world can now be used.

The Analyst's Countertransference

The psychoanalyst has a curious countertransference with this kind of patient. Although the patient represents himself in monstrous terms, the analyst does not experience the patient as viciously destructive. There is a collision between the analyst's sense of the patient and the patient's violent self representations.

I think this instils an unusual caution in the clinician. The discrepancy between the way the analyst experiences the patient and who the patient thinks he is is so vast that I think most clinicians move very cautiously at this point. With James I wondered if I was missing something. We make mistakes with all our patients, and perhaps my sense of this patient's creativity (that is, his actual use of me) was misguided. Was James really a pervert, really psychotic? Did I like him and were these feelings interrupting my judgement? Was I failing the patient?

In a sense, then, my intuitive ability was de-stabilized by the anti-narcissistic self representations. My inner sense – which I rely upon in the formation of interpretations – was called into question. I could not act so much from this part of myself. Wild ideas seemed to get in the way of intuitive accuracy, as the patient vigorously presented fantasies or ideas of himself that confirmed his negative view. But this unconscious disturbance of the analyst's relation to his own inner sense of the patient was a transference recreation of the disturbing effect of a wild or misplaced idea on the child – in James's case, of the mother's grand idea that he was a genius at the age of four. This was experienced by the analyst in the countertransference, as his inner sense of the patient was disturbed by the analysand's intrusive and asynchronous ideas. Like the mother's idea of the child's genius, its negative transfer in analysis (the patient's presentation of the bad self) was more than partly true. Indeed it was the misplaced plausibility of the idea that made it an effective intruder.

The partial truthfulness of the mother's idea is what undermined the child's use of unconscious rapport with her. Partly because of his talent, James was transported from incremental intersubjective maturation (a development sponsored by child–parent mutuality) to precocious dependence on his giftedness. Winnicott wrote about this in another context when discussing the schizoid state which is created by the child's overdependence on mind, as a feature of the false self. The anti-narcissist is, however, infuriated by the loss of rapport with the primary object, and his talent – a feature of the true self potential – is hated.

The patient will transfer this dilemma in analysis by using partly true ideas to disturb the analyst's intuitive sense of him. If the analyst does lose his reliance on his inner senses, then he will have been displaced from the inner core of self, and he will then be at work in a world of misplaced and somewhat useless ideas.

Perhaps it is clear how one of the features of analysis will be the analyst's struggle to sustain (or restore) his inner sense of what is true or false in the patient's representations. He will, of necessity, be at odds with his patient's views, and will find himself conveying a useful incredulity, rather than a useless negativity. Of course, the anti-narcissist will leap upon any comment that seems to suggest his analyst's view of him is guided by the same factors of negation as the patient's own personality, but the analyst's provision of a dialectics, derived in part from his inner sense of what is true, will gradually mitigate the destructive force of wild ideas.

9

The Trauma of Incest

W hat is traumatic about incest? Is it the act itself which violates family or social codes of conventional behaviour? Is it, as Freud suggested, the memory of the event which carries the charge of repressed horrors? Precisely what is it that damages the victim? Is it the physical violation? The mental imagery of the act? The horror of it?

To set this question and others in context, I will provide a very brief vignette which is typical of the course of some victims of a parental molestation. A woman in her twenties, withdrawn, tense, and inhibited, reports in the course of therapy that when she was six her father climbed into bed with her. He would do this after she had fallen asleep. Awakened by his touches, she then feigned sleep as he rubbed his penis against her. Eventually a relative discovered the father in the act, and he was exiled from the family. The mother and daughter moved from the countryside to a city, and lived on the poverty line for many years. The girl found herself then totally dependent on the mother whom she described as a very tough woman. Indeed, she seemed preoccupied in her therapy sessions with many accounts of her mother's coldness and harshness, and only occasionally did she ever talk about the father and the incest.

This picture of the mother is not so unusual when working with victims of incest. Why does the daughter preoccupy herself with the mother, a woman whom she characterized as a tough almost masculine figure? Was the mother's unnurturing masculine personality a contributing factor to this child's fate, insofar as the father had to seek sexual 'intimacy' elsewhere? Does the father's act represent a penetration committed by the mother? After all, she accepts him in marriage, leaves her daughter in his care, and is therefore in a sense responsible for his violation of her child. How else, it is proposed, can we explain the abused child's subsequently fraught relation to the mother, which is so often an intrinsic part of this situation?

A woman may marry a man who is attractive because of a selective and intense infantile impulsiveness, and it is possible that in bearing his child, and then in leaving a daughter to him to molest, the mother is a crucial partner in the pathway to child abuse. Were this the case, then we could focus on how the mother fails the child's early infantile needs and quietly shoves the child and the father together for a rendezvous of secret, stolen pleasures.

All this is possible, and a clinician needs to keep an open mind. I can only say that in my clinical experience I have never come across the above dynamic. How else may we understand the child's distressed relation to a phallic mother?

The Father's De-structuring of His Function

In a sense, when the father commits an act of incest, he de-structures the child's relation to himself as the father. At this moment he is no longer the *father*, as he has broken the law of 'the Name of the Father' (Lacan, 1977, p. 218) by acting in a different name. Instead, he acts in the name of the mother, or more accurately, he re-presents the body of the mother, and annihilates the phallus as an intrapsychic object that facilitates the child's evolution to independence. The phallus signifies the not–mother, and identification with it helps the child to emerge from the pre-oedipal relation to the mother. The victim of incest, however, finds herself cast back into the relation to mother, the early mother of the first three years of life. Such a casting is a temporal trauma, a warp of time, as the child is transported into a past life. From this psychic time-warp (which differs from a fixation), she re-experiences the mother. And who will this mother be? She is already very different from the original mother, insofar as **the father has entered the child's bed under licence from the body of the mother, only now, with the body of a mother bearing his penis**.

Why is the molesting father the body of the mother? I imagine this to be so, because the father exploits the child's recent experience to gain access to the child's bed and body. It is an error to claim that the child wishes the father to commit his act of incest. I think his fatherliness, especially as an erotic factor, rests in his upholding his name, partly accomplished by keeping his body distant from the child's body, and thus facilitating the child's need to separate from body-to-body intimacy. The father builds on that generative absence first created by the mother when she goes away from the infant and returns. In some respects, as the infant imagines, she goes into the father's world (the away spaces, the distance, the separateness) and returns. To father as distance and back to the dialectic of bodies.

When the father commits incest, he enters the psychic skin of the mother. It has been her place to lie with her infant, to give it suck, to cuddle its body against her, the first pillow for the infant's sleep. In this respect, then, the mother is unconsciously viewed as a criminal partner in molestation, because the father has entered the mother's body and exploited the mother–child relation in order to gain access to the child. And the child feels very confused and guilty, because she admits the father to the bed through the mother's licence, which is indeed a certain crime against the mother, an abuse of the mother's generatively restrained managing of body-to-body relations.

The victim of an incest, then, tends to recall the masculine qualities of the mother, because it is this mother–father that the father was when he committed the act. One of the unconscious shared secrets of this rendezvous is that it represents the undoing of the father, and the presentation of an impotent man, a 'mummy man' who feebly seeks to share his penis as an object of co-victimization. When the child is subsequently left with the mother, with the father de-structured, she creates a phallic mother for two reasons. First, because this is the confusing after-image of the father. It is her way of specifying the confusion of the father's act. Second, she tries to find the phallus in the mother, in order to discover a psychic structure that will enable her to be differentiated from the mother's body and body-relating. One of the traumatic effects of the father's crime is to send the child back into a confused relation to the mother, as the father vaporizes his structural function through his mummification of himself, and the child concentrates on the mother's phallic qualities in order to discover a differentiating structure. This is why I think that some victims of incest often talk more about the mother's personality and the relation to the mother than they do about the father's abuse.

If the victim can only congregate an image of a weak mother, it is likely that this objectifies her capitulation to the regressed terms of the time warp. She is stuck inside a weak and structureless 'mummy world'.

Topographic Reversal

What does it mean to go to bed, to fall asleep, perhaps to dream, to be awakened by the father's sexual presence? Of course, the father is one of the primary libidinal objects. So this is an occasion of the actual object's arrival for its sexual usage by the child but not in accordance with the child's present wishes. The father's act reverses the direction of the child's sexual desire. The libidinal object says, 'Here I am to use your wishes for me', which constitutes a topographic reversal of instinctual life. The topographic model charts the journey of the soma's urges as they demand mental representation in the curious parliamentary world of the unconscious. When the urge finds an object through which it can find at least a partial gratification, then its journey ends in the discharge of excitation. But this ever-recurring process has other important mental functions as it educates the preconscious in the value of symbolic life and in the acculturation of the unconscious ego that finds the objects of displacement for the soma's urge.

If we think of a young girl asleep, some of her dreams will represent this process with the father as the object of her urges. Perhaps this will lead to a direct representation of him in the dream as a sexual object, but more likely the unconscious ego will disguise the wish and the object in that compromise necessary to allow the dream representation. From the soma to the mind. This is the direction of the topography.

But if the father invades the child's bed, he becomes an object that seeks the child's body (and somatic response) for his purposes. The child is then in the grip of a topographical reversal as the object of desire ruins the valence of topographic representation; what was to have been the relieving terminal of excitation becomes a counter-movement of uncontrolled excitement moving backward – in reverse – from symbolic representation, to mental presentation, to soma.

The effect of this topographical reversal is to alarm the psyche about the consequences of processing wishes and to sponsor a selective deletion of subsequent representations. Important mental processes, such as condensation and displacement, which are vital factors in the child's formation of symbols and expression of unconscious life through play are denuded. The topographic reversal creates a circumscribed secret paranoia. The child remains hidden from her desires, as she fears that desiring betrays the location of the true self and invites further topographic destruction. I wish to stress that the secret paranoia of the abused child is not a suspicion of the father or of men, although this may be how it is presented. The paranoia is a fear of a reversal of psychic processes which is intrapsychically and personally damaging. The dread is of further denudation of mental processes, not simply a fear of being touched by the father. It is not the body that is the true victim of this violation. The crime, as we know, is the abuse of the mind and self.

No Place of Rest

If the father's incest institutes a topographic reversal, as a libidinal object seeking its source of gratification in the child's psyche-soma, then this violation of the child is also an attack on the dream and dreaming. If he is the object of the child's desire, then he is meant to be 'inside' the dream space, not in the outside actual world. Each child abused in the night must wonder, 'Is this a dream?', 'Is this really happening?' We know that the dream is an extraordinarily efficient psychic act. It filters the symbolically rich events of the day to contact earlier historical experiences in order to sustain the person's creative relation to facts of life. When the father penetrates this space, I think he electrifies the dream process, so that from this moment on dreaming bears an anxiety, an alarm that this procedure is not truly deeply inside one, not safe enough to escape the penetration of reality.

The child then cannot feel secure in distinguishing the dream from reality, an inability that charges dreaming with an anxiety state that often wakes the dreamer up in a nightmare. In this respect a nightmare is the dreamer's psychotic panic over not being able to distinguish the dream from reality. It's the moment when the dreamer feels that the dream is real, that she is caught up inside reality, and so must wake into the actual world to find relief. This is a reversal of the place of rest. The non-anxious dreamer sleeps to rest, while the victim of the nightmare cannot find rest anywhere.

If the victim of child abuse brings into adult life (and hence into analysis) a dread of dreaming that either impoverishes her inner symbolic life or informs the dream process with a chronic charge of anxiety, then she also bears with her an inability to experience reverie. The dream process plays an important part in the developmental construction of internal psychic space, but this internal space (where we dream, imagine, talk to ourselves, and think) for the incest victim is not experienced as a good container which can transform the experience of life into nurturing psychic material. The victim of a molestation, therefore, may be deeply paralysed as a container, unable to experience that reverie essential to the transformation of experience into reflectiveness. Thus this person will have some disability in learning from analytic experience, and the psychoanalyst will note that she has an aversion to entertaining psychoanalytic objects (the analyst's interpretation) because she does not possess a good enough container.

Fearing Psychoanalysis

To my way of thinking, this is the most pernicious feature of the trauma of sexual abuse. The child not only cannot find true rest, but, dreading psychic processing of the elements of life, is therefore impoverished in the construction of the psyche and in the experience of reverie. This, of course, bears immediately upon the victim's experience of a psychoanalysis. Analysis is not experienced as useful. It is experienced as an attack on the person's self, as an organized system of expectation that only emphasizes the person's inadequacy and separation from human life. Perhaps this explains why some victims associate analysis with molestation. They may run from analysis into another form of treatment as they experience the analyst as harming them. Why? Can we say simply that they experience the analyst as seducing them? If this does seem to be a significant element of the accusation, then how is this so? How is the analyst imagined in this way, and why is this not also the case with the supportive psychotherapist?

It should be made clear that it is not the analyst per se who constitutes this second molestation, but the factors of analysis. The analytic silence simply announces the sleep that is no sleep, a silence–sleep that does not lead to reverie but to an electrifying fear. The distant body of the analyst withheld from the patient's senses (of sight and intersubjective kinetics) excites the memory of the attack on the mental apparatus. This person does not want to experience sexual feelings and personal need emerging from within and directed towards the analyst–father. The situation itself is the scene of the original seduction, a kind of *déjà-vu* that is overwhelming. One of the person's fears is that if she were to relax into the analytic situation, and to rest, then at the point when she can represent needs and desires, the libidinal object will intrude, exploit her psyche–soma, and create a topographic reversal that is not simply experienced as the object's paradoxical suppression of her desire, but, more importantly, as a de-structuring of the psychic processes essential to living.

How can the analyst approach this situation without unwittingly treading on the patient's mind? I believe that the analyst needs to put the nature of this transference experience of the analytic process into words as soon as possible. Analytic silence may require the following comments: 'Perhaps this silence feels "eerie"'; or, 'This silence does not feel restful'; or 'The silence leaves you tense and wondering "What is this man up to?"' Analytic interpretation may inspire subsequent comments by the analyst such as, 'I can see that you feel "jolted" by my comment'; or, 'This may be another moment when you feel "oh oh, what's he up to now? What does he expect of me?"' Or, 'Oh God, what am I to do with this man's statements?' The patient's claustrophobic anxiety panics need to be taken up immediately: 'Oh no! I can't think in here! I have no mind here! I'm blank! Let me out of this crazy place'; or, 'He's just asked me something. He's waiting for my reply. He wants something from me. I've got to get out of here!' The patient's anger with mental processes themselves needs repeated work: 'God damn it. I don't want to think about these things!' Or, 'Now, there you go again, thinking about perfectly ordinary things I've talked to you about. Why don't you just be quiet!' Or, 'You fool. You are a fool. Only fools think that thinking helps!'

The victim's contempt for the analytic process reflects an understandable compensatory contempt for her own mental processes. We can understand how the patient needs to shut out her mind, and therefore how she must refuse analysis as well. It is one of the painful, though liberating, ironies of analytic work with such a person that she simply wishes to announce the act of having been abused as if this is sufficient to explain or to represent the trauma of sexual abuse. But the trauma of abuse is not, as we know, conveyed by the account of the act. Indeed, more often than not, the victim of parental molestation will describe the act in either somewhat vague or uncertain terms, or in a startlingly matter-of-fact manner. The true representation of the trauma, of the effect of the father's dismantling of the law of the phallus, is in the victim's confused states of mind, which enact an unconscious time–warp of being back with the mother, and in her somewhat empty phallic identifications which signify her effort to organize the mother into a father segment that allows her separation from her small child self's mother. This confusion is lived out without the benefit of reflective mental work, because the patient has a dread of dreaming and no experience of reverie, thus truly impoverishing her in her ability to work her way through her distress. This will manifest itself in an initial inability to make use of psychoanalysis and an immediate interpretation of the analytic process as a dementing seduction.

However, through the analyst's interpretation of the patient's experiences of the analytic process and the analyst in the here and now, the patient is gradually able to tolerate the analytic procedure. Indeed, analytic interpretation of the transference constitutes a transformation of the patient's acute dread – akin to a beta experience of an undigested fact – into alpha elements that construct a contact barrier (restoring the mind) and assist the patient in rebuilding a psyche that feels adequate to think the thoughts of life.

At the same time, this partnership in rebuilding the psyche enables the analysand to entertain needs and sexual wishes and to experience an actual object as a libidinal possibility. The actual object can be introjected and sexually cathected precisely because of the analyst's preservation of his distance. In this respect, I think that a simply supportive psychotherapy constituted out of reassurances will only restore the patient's relation to a good enough mother, but will not necessarily restore the relation to the father.

A Countertransference

Writing this chapter has actually constituted a working through of a countertransference that I have to the sexually abused woman, and it is to this issue, and to the necessity of Freud's two theories of hysteria that I now turn.

A countertransference. I receive into my consulting room a young woman in her twenties. She is interesting looking, and as she tells me about her depressions and current life situation, I think of this as a promising situation for analysis. In the second session, the patient is uncomfortably silent. She seems to have given up making any effort to engage me or to tell me anything further about herself. She stares at the floor. I mention that she seems different today. She replies that there is something she has not told me and that it is the reason why she has come for help. I can feel my heart sinking slightly. No one comes to analysis for one single reason. Such a complaint itself is symptomatic of an impoverishment. The patient describes a sexual molestation and then looks up, and that is that! The rest is up to me. My heart has now sunk out of sight. When I am in such a situation I usually think, 'Oh, no! Not that', or 'Well, that's the end of an interesting prospect', or some such response.

I believe this 'confession' of a transgression creates in the analyst's mind the very essence of the trauma of molestation. As I feel, 'Well, that's the end of that' and 'Well, what now', I reflect the despair over a loss of reflective thought. Ostensibly I feel this because as the patient asserts that she was violated, this has to be accepted as the undisputed source of her problem. I know the patient will scrutinize me for any signs of disbelief, and I know I don't wish to be involved in any internal adjudication over whether this really happened or didn't. And why not? Because my mind gets taken up with litigious factors, inside an imaginary courtroom, which distracts me from my patient and makes the person one-dimensional. And yet this is seemingly what she wants. She demands that I take her at face value.

In a sense, the victim passes the act on to the analyst who may feel that he has lost his right to analyse just as the patient has lost her right to dream, to play, and to desire. The fact of an act is conveyed with a certain weight, decentring the analyst from his person as an analyst, and bearing the patient's transfer of the fact of transgression which also weighed so heavily in her life that she could not get back in her own mind.

I know I always feel a depression when I hear this news, and this mood is not, I confess, an act of empathy. It is not because I feel sorrow for the victim. Instead, I am disappointed over the (apparent) ending of the analytic. I am out of work. Redundant. Relegated to the dole of psychotherapy. And I am angry that this has happened to me. Again, it is fruitful to consider how my response to this news is, in my view, similar to the despair and fury of the victim of incest. When the father violates the child, the child can no longer play with this father in her mind. He terminates the imaginary. Just as the patient's heavy declaration ends my right to imagine my patient in many ways, to reflect on many issues, to get lost on tangents of speculation, to play with representations. No! I must stick to the fact: the actual event. It is to dominate, control, and centre the analysis. This transfer is startlingly close to the patient's experience of the father's abuse.

The father's seduction of the daughter breaches the child's ordinary processing of bodily instincts to their objects of desire. By instituting a topographic reversal, he invests actual objects with a sexually unruly potential, and the child will live in unconscious fear of the effect of the other's desire. The violation is to mental processing, and the victim will carry this insidious paradigm in her, as she divests interrelating of its imaginative potential.

10

'Don't Worry Your Father'

W hat does it mean when a mother says this to her children?
Manifestly, of course, we know she says, 'Keep this to
ourselves; we don't wish to overburden the father'. But
what are the psychic states represented and potentialized through this
comment? I shall approach this question from several different
positions.

What if this speech accurately expresses the father's communication to the mother? Assume he has either told her he does not want
bad news, or that, when he comes home from work, he does not want
to hear anything stressful. We know that situation in which the
returning father yells out, 'I have enough trouble at work, and now
you tell me this!' The scene suggests an apologetic wife, and children
hidden away but within earshot of the father's remark.

It's Off To Work We Go...

W hat does this domestic moment suggest, if we wonder about its
psychic status in the minds of the participants? The father has
been away at 'work', the place of true labour, of necessary effort. This
place is economically significant and the father may encourage the
family to believe that this 'supports' the family – which is true up to a
point. The 'home' is intended to be his alternative space, his 'home
sweet home', where he is to find comfort and certainly no more work.
After all, now he is no longer on the job. Work is for money, and the
problems of the family yield no further income. Does one ask the
father for off-duty labour, without double pay?

Indeed, not only does this tax the father's patience – this

out-of-place labour – it also threatens the economic well-being of the family unit. This is suggested by the notion of an overworked man capable of a psycho-mechanical breakdown, which would then push the family unit into poverty. There is a foreboding sense in this potential economic disenfranchisement of the family. They do not have the economic right to expect this of the father, who assigns himself the role of the one who solves problems for money.

Of course, the above is only one type of father, but I shall keep him as a target of my oedipally-driven analysis a bit longer. At this point in the mother's representation of the child's problem, or problem child, to the father, the mother relies upon the passage of time – an interval between the father's arrival from work to his home. In this scene, she has already told her children prior to the father's arrival that at first no one must present the accumulated stresses of the house space to the father who was working in the other area.

The two areas of work, the one in which one is labouring through the day for money, the other where one is absent and problems accrue, constitute two psychic structures. The one is the world of men and income, the other the space of children, mothers, and expenditure. The family spends *while* the father earns.

There is a *split* between the two areas:

1.   Work and income outside the home
2.   Expenditure, unpaid labour inside the home.

To present the father with home problems is to drain him, to further sap his strength, a potency now that is somehow sustained by his work in the other place.

Who is the father at this moment? Or shall we say what is this? Bear in mind that in posing this question I assume that this father is an actual presence and an internal object, so the scene described has internal object significance, and, indeed, may constitute a psychic stance: an invariant process always present even when not used.

Internally, 'Don't worry your father' becomes another statement, now intrapsychic: 'Don't take any more from your father who has been away so that we might spend (live)'. Indeed, it is often said of him that he 'earns a living' or that he has a 'livelihood': a concept that links the economic life of the father to life itself.

The Father Machine

I s life itself threatened by worrying the father? Well, certainly this would appear to be the case if the presentation of problems caused an overload in the father who burst, like a broken machine, now disabled from working in the place of labour. The 'outburst' of his rage, a phrase that emphasizes the father as machine, threatens the life of the family who may now be without livelihood: no shelter, no clothing, no food. May we say that psychically to worry the father is to break the money machine and to bring about starvation?

Who or what has the father become in this other place, to become capable of an outburst? What wisdom is there in the mother's caution to the children to let time pass, often accompanied by further reminders: 'Now be sure to run up to him and say hello or give him a hug. And tell him how well you did at school. But then leave him alone, and wait until after dinner to tell him your problems'?

An interesting sequence this. He needs a greeting, some affection, and good news of the happenings in this other (alternative) space where he hasn't been, but which is one of the two essential spaces of his life. May we say that the scenario prepared by the playwright–mother partly aims to give the father the right idea of the goings-on in this other space? The inhabitants welcome him and inform him that all news is good news. Then they disappear to leave him alone until after he is fed.

Again we must wonder what this person is who requires such treatment? In any event, as the father is left to read the paper, to watch some television, to read a magazine, a transition of sorts is occurring. The father is no longer at work nor quite yet in the family, but somewhere in between. Is a newspaper a transitional object (not in Winnicott's sense, however), there for the father in the in-between state?

But perhaps the father has had this transition period of sorts when sitting on the train and by the time he is home has arrived already at the next stage of evolution in daily destiny. Maybe he is now ready to 'chat' with his wife about his day at work, or her day at home. Although a crisis in both lives may affect this scene – so that mother or father may go straight to the crisis – ordinarily they both chat.

What is the status of this event for the children as this process is repeated day after day? Well, the father is in transition from being a money-making person, and somewhat mechanical (capable of out-burst), to becoming Daddy. To achieve this he needs a special greeting, time to himself, and a chat with the mother. There is an idea, then, of a change taking place within him, a movement from one personality to another, from wage–earner to Daddy.

Is it not possible, then, that the child imagines the mother's structuring of the relation to the father as essential to the *humanizing* of the father, so that there is no premature relating to the father–worker, which would burst the machine and destroy the family's livelihood? The concept here is that the pre-transitional father is not humanized sufficiently to process the conflicts in this other space. The mother, with the assistance of the children, facilitates the evolution of the father toward his new self, and after dinner, she picks the moment to tell him of the worries.

Although few may recognize their families in the above script, I am not aiming at sociological analysis, but at something else: the psychic status of the phrase, 'Don't worry your father'. It is common enough so that its other contexts (including the mother as wage-earner) may be substituted for the one I give.

Home Again

P art of the humanization of the father is the transition to emotional reality, to its terms, in the movement from work space to home life. A mother or child may interrupt this transition to present a worry, but it may only fetch a smile and a 'What a shame' response. In other words, the father has heard the worry but not engaged with it. So we may view this scene from another angle: the need of the mother. Having 'contained' much of the distress of the day (of school news, neighbourhood life, and so on), the mother needs to tell the father about the details in order to partly pass on the containing process to the father. So her instruction to the children about the father is also to serve her need for his transition to container. If the children prematurely tell the father, he may either blow up, or, what is perhaps worse, he may hear the news only at an intellectual level and not accept his psychic responsibility to share the burden of 'home–work'.

So preparing the father for this psychic responsibility is a difficult task for the mother. The father may come home as the worker–

machine, labouring for a livelihood, and in need now of peace and quiet. At such a moment he is in no mood for any further conflict, and the mother's management of the father is crucial in his transition toward psychic responsibility.

I do not wish to labour this idea. Obviously, some men arrive home to immediately inquire about how everyone is and be ready for 'home–work', and then there are some who want to hear nothing at all.

The transformation of the father, a domestic ritual of everyday life, of course has psychic consequences. At the very least it suggests that this other place where the father works is a reality which harbours no space for the father's psychic containment of the family. Reality, at least this reality, must be transformed into something else. The child, then, may have a curious relation to the father's other space. At once vital to life, it does not allow for the child's psychic use of the father. It is therefore a rather impersonal or harsh space, a place of essential no–admittance, an area of labour. The father is both representative of the family in this space and the bearer of the traces of this other world back to the family, who learn that unless he is allowed a humanizing decompression chamber, he will feel ruptured by the transition from work to home.

The family's relation to the other father (of work) and the nature of his transformation into Daddy is of considerable psychic importance to the growing child. To some extent this is essential preparatory work in the child's relation to reality, which perhaps seems – as it is – a space beyond the child's capabilities just as much as the father's phallic equipment is superior to the child's. And, as the father therefore has a genital ability to gain the mother sexually, so too does he have another ability to move into reality.

What is this other factor, from which the child is excluded? What is its mental status in the father and the child? Perhaps it's wise to consider this in terms of a reverse transformation: the father 'off to work'. Up early, before the others, he showers, shaves, applies some after-shave, gets dressed, and briskly eats his breakfast. What is the law of this moment? It is *time*. The time to go to work. Time to meet the march of time itself: to move off, to get to work *on time*. This element is, of course, also a feature of the mother's and children's lives, but there is a period before the children go to school when the father embodies this time in the home. He founds this law of time and it carries the members of the family out and away from the home space.

Those who live by this time are carried off by it to the other place – the world of work and tasks. And how different *this* transition is from the father's undoing of such time as destiny when he 'unwinds' at home, aiming to come out of time. In the morning he is winding himself up, heading away, energized, for time.

The father's return from work, then, is a complex intrapsychic moment for the child who awaits him, for the wife who may have to process him, and for the man himself. The return of the father from the other place is suffused with projective potential, as for the child this other place is, in some respects, the domain of the unconscious itself. But it is not the space for dreaming, an interior space, the remnant of life *in utero*, but a space for an unconscious use of the real. I am suggesting, here, that unconscious mental work differs according to that psychic moment during which it ocurs. The ego 'knows' the dream space. This area can be used for a complex living out of identifications across time and space. The ego knows the oedipal space, and the child's wakeful musings, derived from desire, will reflect unconscious knowledge of the range of unconscious scenarios. Equally, the other place, to which the father goes, is a mental area in the child, a potential projective location, that will elicit and store the child's unconscious interpretation of the father in that space.

Two Areas of the Mind

Thus when the father returns home, a transition also occurs in the child's mind, as there is an intrapsychic shift of the father from the work area (in life and in psyche) to the home (in life and psyche). Therefore, 'Don't worry your father', aimed to nurture the father from one place to another, is shadowed by an internal shift aimed at helping the child to demarcate or separate the two areas of the mind, and to find a different use of time to suit the needs of the self. I mean that this time serves the self (time for personal transition), while the march of time in the mornings is the dictate of a more powerful force: the social order.

Clinical work with children sometimes reveals a preoccupation with the safety of the father, both at work and particularly while being transported home. In some ways it reflects the child's concern that the father is damaged by the daily transformation to the other place, a projection of the child's mutilation anxiety on to the father, biased here by an ego itself incapable of handling the transition to work. Indeed, going to school is an important part of this ego accomplishment and can be viewed as ego training in the technique of moving from psychic life in one part of the mind (the home) to another part of the mind (work). The infant will already have had an earlier ego schooling in transitions: from the womb to the outside world, from attachment to the mother to separation, and so forth.

Thus, if a child is inordinately worried about the father's safety, we must consider the possibility that he is objectifying his terror about successfully establishing an inner space that houses the self going off to the other place (the not-home). The reasons why the child may be unable to do this are too numerous to itemize. They could reflect a family incapacity to send the father 'off to work' in a good way and to receive him back with a welcome. They could reflect earlier conflicts that have rendered the child's psychic structure weak, making it difficult for the child to imagine the father in the other place. Or, of course, his oedipal strivings, the wish to kill the father, may show up in the child's fear for the father's safety. After all, Laius was killed on the road!

A child in psychotherapy fears for his father's safety on the journey home from work. It is his primary symptom. He is reading *The Odyssey* at school and associates the journey taken by Odysseus as a metaphor for his journey with the female therapist. Yet he says that if Odysseus destroys his return home and 'the search for his family' still 'in this way he fulfils his curiosity...'

Times of our Life

N ow what does this child teach us, about what we may term the Odysseus complex? Does he not imply that the father may fail to return to the family because, his task completed, the father now wishes to fulfil his curiosity. In this complex the child projects his pregenital polymorphous sexuality into the father who wanders off, driven by the winds of curiosities, his psychic responsibility to his family strangely gone from his mind. And to this projection the child may later add a more organized oedipal element: that the father, harassed by the child and the mother, will wander off to a more welcoming place.

This Odysseus complex suggests another function to the injunctive, 'Don't worry your father. Don't worry him, or he will not come home. We will not see him here, but will only hear of his voyages elsewhere.' And in modern society, a man is likely to wander off driven by a sense of home abuse: of being failed by the home space.

At a certain point in his life the child awaits the father's return from that other world. Until then he or she has lived in a world distinguished by its seeming timelessness. There are certain senses of time, of somatic time and object relational time. The soma determines its hunger: time for a feed. The bladder holds its contents up to a point: time to urinate. The infant feels drowsy: time to sleep. The object (mother) participates in the infant's somatic time by gratifying urges, as in a breast feed, or in managing needs, as when she puts him in a restful position for sleep. But she also introduces another time, the object's time, as, for example, when she walks away from the infant, into another room, leaving him with her absence, and a sense of the passing of time linked to the coming and going of the object. When the mother goes away, perhaps simply to another room, the infant experiences time passing as the presence of maternal absence. A source of anxiety, this untimely departure can become a source of amusement to the child if the mother plays with time. She must hide for a moment and then reappear. The lapse of seconds becomes a thrill.

Even if the infant uses these senses of time to gather together experiences of anticipation or reflection, he lives in a fundamentally timeless world. The mother will sustain for a while that sense of no time (of no where, no place) that comes out of the neonate's prior progressions, from unaliveness to aliveness, from predependent aloneness, to its birth into the object world. Even as the infant experiences early senses of time, he will still live within a world that makes few demands on his time, that suspends itself to accommodate his needs, that materializes objects to gratify infant pleasure. Perhaps the laws of the unconscious – its instinctual basis, its amorality, its timelessness – owe their making to the mother and that world she creates for her infant. Ferenczi (1938) said that intercourse represents a phylogenetic wish, as the man's penis represents our urge to return to that sea from which we originated, a sea now maintained in the body of the woman. Is it possible that the unconscious is what we carry in ourself of those primordial years of our existence, when we emerge out of unaliveness into aliveness? Is not the dream a likely kin to the perceptual world of the infant, in that instinctual requirements and objects have an immediate relation to one another? The dream, as Pontalis (1981) has said, is the body of the mother; we crawl into it at night; we collude with the night by darkening our wakeful perceptiveness; we enter a world of endless possibilities.

When the mother goes away to prepare a meal (a few minutes), to go shopping (an hour), or to bear another child (a few days), she marries another time. This is the time that orders the father, who marches to it in the morning and unwinds from it at night. One of the child's tasks is to find a creative integration of these two orders of time. This object time, that sense of temporality created by the mother's movements, is a precursor to the father's affiliation with his march to time. She is transitional between the infant's somatic time (to which she attends and marches) and the immutable time of the fathers who have set the clocks of social movement. Her capacity to mediate between these two times has an almost transcendent quality to it, as if she carries within her touches of timeless eternality that come with bearing aliveness out of nowhere.

The other day, while at the seaside, I watched a father kicking a football with his son on the beach. The boy could only have been about two. I was astonished at how ably he fielded the ball, how deftly he stopped it, tapped a short punt of a few yards, then ran up and gave it an accurate kick. He was concentrating absolutely on the ball and on the place of the father. But in the intervening seconds, when the ball was met and returned by the father, the child found time to gaze at objects in the sand, often to turn away completely from his father. Perhaps the time sense of rhythm itself brought his attention back to the football game. I wondered if this other world wasn't the place of daydream and that other order of time: the maternal space that permits imagination and reverie.

I am reminded of my own childhood, those days at primary school, when I would leave my task-oriented concentration and wander off into the world of daydream. There I could be a hero. Or anything. In the schoolroom I was bound by the tiresome reminder of actual ignorance.

At some point in his life the child becomes intensely aware of the father's affiliation with the timeful, i.e., the not–timeless. The father lives, or so it seems, in a different order of time, as I have discussed, one we could call paternal time, to distinguish it from maternal time.

Maternal time:		Paternal time:	
1.	timeless	1.	timeful
2.	instinctual	2.	social
3.	eternal	3.	mortal
4.	intimate	4.	impersonal

We have these two time senses in us. We begin in maternal time, and the infant–mother relation is the intersubjective ground for the formation of the laws of the unconscious. The mother introduces us to the father and contains elements of paternal time when she separates from the infant. She creates a transition to the other time sense, as she sustains the illusion for the infant that his need is her time and that she will return from the away space according to the infant's demand.

But the father does not. Indeed he must not be disturbed in his daily routine, as he departs from the family. We could say that there are some children who cannot make this transition to integration with paternal time. Perhaps oedipal aggression is too successful, as the child disposes of the father. Or the mother prefers to keep the child in her timeless world. Or the husband disavows his own timefulness and the child has inadequate assistance to meet up with the paternal time.

To maternal timelessness and paternal timefulness we may add a third order of a child's time: that of his own biological development. Each year of a child's development is marked by body changes as the child grows into his future. Biological time has its own destiny, and the small girl knows one day her body will be ready to conceive children, as the small boy also knows that some time in the future the body will enable him to penetrate and impregnate a woman. We know children do not simply evolve biologically; they also evolve psychologically in what we term psycho–development. If we combine the factors of psychic and biological evolution, we have what we might term psycho-biological time, which forms a third temporal order.

The Child who Worries about the Father's Transportation

When the child worries about the safety of the father during transportation from work to home, he objectifies his fear both of the father's capacity to cross time zones, but also of his own ability to enter historical time without damage to the self. Each child certainly comes to sense that there is a world, making its history, marching to its time, beyond the walls of home. Much as the infant might wish to preserve the mother's creation of timelessness, he eventually realizes he is being asked to enter history: first, as a novice, to study the grammar, maths, literature, and society of the timeful world; and second, as the post-adolescent: to make some place for himself in time, perhaps even, to make his mark. The child's recognition of the timeful is not an abstract realization, as the psycho-biological time is the body's movement to its schedule of change. A reluctant child, then, is destined to change, driven by time.

Daydreaming may well be an intermediate time, between the timeless, the timeful, and biological time. It follows the laws of the timeless (as the child can transport himself); it gives expression to the events of biological development as the child will partly dream from instinctual urges and ego needs; but it also takes place 'in' the timeful, as the child comes 'back to' reality and history.

The child who worries about the father's transportation metaphorizes his own difficulty in integrating the three times. Father, who will be harmed or lost, carries the child's projection of an endangered part of the self that feels vulnerable because the three orders of time cannot be brought into harmony with one another. Presumably the father is also the heroic figure who is meant to pass through time zones (his own, timelessness, and timefulness) without damage. At home, unwound, he enters a timeless temporality, a figure of eternity, joining the other infinities of character: mother and child. Through ritual in the morning (shower, breakfast, getting dressed) he moves from dream and timelessness to join the movement of history. Does Faust not aim to escape this timefulness, to cross historical evolution in a timeless carriage of wish and whimsy? Is this transgression not the cause of a terrible day of reckoning, as surely he has killed the father (the timeful) to marry the mother's order and thereby to occupy the father's territory under the mother's terms? Perhaps the Faust

191

legend expresses the wishes and fears of the oedipal child who would like to exercise the omnipotence at hand in the world of maternal time, in order to slay the father, and prematurely realize his future.

In childhood, a young person-in-formation lives in an intermediate world between the timeless and the timeful. In playing he expresses his place in a series of external actions, lived out on his terms, in a holding environment (the home or garden). In daydreaming he plays internally, often because he is in another space that is timeful: a school, driving in a car. His primary assistance is his own biological time that destines him to move through childhood into adulthood, although he is also identified with the mother's progressive mediation between several orders of time.

In our adult lives we continue to mediate the nature of these different temporal orders. Timelessness and timefulness marry up increasingly through memory, as we link the two orders in what we call the past: a place relating to the timeless and the timeful. And our body time, due to the unwinding of its progressions, eventually informs us of that death which shall be the final time, perhaps that one moment when all the orders of time recognize and unite into one.

11

Historical Sets and the Conservative Process

One of the casualties of the present intense interest in the 'here and now' transference interpretation is the diminution of the 'there and then'. It is maintained that, as all perception is selective, there is no registration of the actuality of family life, only the subject's personal experience of the actual world. Furthermore, any recollection of the past must be viewed as a phantastical reading that reflects present-day internal object relations, so recollecting the past only serves the selective aims of the present. Since a patient thinking of his history does so in the presence of the analyst, such historical considerations must be regarded as unconscious representations of the patient's present experience of the analyst. The point is often stressed that all that we can truly know anyway is the present experience, the precise nature of how the patient relates to us and constitutes us in his inner world, and how we experience the presence of the analysand. To go beyond this immediate experience, whether we try to think with the analysand about some distress in present-day relations, or aim to reflect on his childhood, is to leave the immediacy of the analyst–analysand interaction. To consider contemporary issues or the past is to collude with the patient's splitting of the transference and to accept the projective identification of the elements of the transference into the narrative objects that refer to persons and events external to the analytic relationship. To avoid this mutual enactment, the analyst must firmly hold his ground and only interpret the patient's material and behaviour as it speaks his ego's relation to the analyst–object.

The accomplishment of this rigorous point of view is one of the most significant contributions of the British school of Psychoanalysis – and particularly the Klein group – to the practice of contemporary psychoanalysis. The stress on the primacy of the here and now as the core of the analysis is, in my view, the most important therapeutic advance in British technique since the discovery in the 1940s and 1950s (Heimann, 1956; Racker, 1957) of the precise object relational significance of the countertransference. In particular, by understanding the patient's narrative as a metaphor of the patient's ego experience of the analytic object, the clinician was suddenly alive in a field of meaningful plenty. An analysand who previously was just mumbling about mundane and superficial events from the humdrum cupboards of domesticity was in fact talking about no such thing. The analysand was, in fact, an unconsciously gifted metaphorist and the analyst could simply translate any of these terms to himself or to the patient as expressions of present-day interest. If Freud liberated the hysteric from the dungeons of medical bias, if Klein and Rosenfeld (along with Sullivan) divested the schizophrenics of the label of unanalysability, the British analysts of the 1940s freed the boring patient from the analyst's narcoleptic countertransference.

Now some thirty years after the diffusion of the idea that narrative material is a continuous extended metaphor of the present experience, it has become absolutely essential (at least in London) when reporting one's clinical work to demonstrate exactly how one has transformed a patient's narrative or behaviour into a here and now transference interpretation. But vital as this clinical stance is, I think it has led to the neglect of another important and previously valued clinical function: the need to collect together the details of a patient's history and to link him to his past in a way that is meaningful.

How do we respond to those objections put forward to the use of history in psychoanalysis? We can never know what truly happened and we remember events for bogus reasons. Why then think historically?

Ego Structure as Memory

In the first place, I believe we do have some representations of the actuality of our infant–child experience. Here I stress the actual world and its registration more than I do the child's phantastical renderings of it.

In my view (Bollas, 1987), infants do internalize the mother's actual idiom of care, which is a complex network of 'rules for being and relating'. These rules are procedures for processing internal and external reality, and their regularity eventually leads to their structuring in the ego. Of course this infant–mother interaction is a dialectic as the infant's true self negotiates with the mother's unconscious logic of care. Within her care system are complex assumptions about being and relating and the establishment of this logic becomes part of that deep structure that is the 'grammar of the ego' (Bollas, 1987).

Isn't ego structure a form of memory, and its structure a testimony to the logic of its formation rather like a building recollects an architect's intent? (Bollas, 1987) If so, this type of memory is operational and structural and not representational and recollective.

Infants encode the actual world in their ego: it becomes part of them. And this actuality of the real mother is not an artifice of phantasy; it is not merely the work of the drives. I do not think, however, that it is possible for the psychoanalyst to distinguish easily between the person's registration of the actual and his representation of the aims of the true self via a distortion of the real.

What are we to do if we hold this view? I certainly do not think the analyst should throw his hands up in the air and conclude that this proves he can never know what really happened. The fact that it is true that we cannot ever know what actually happened for sure is not equivalent to the statement that nothing of the actual is present in the patient's memory or in the transference. I do think the patient's conveying of the actual events, the mother's and father's logic of handling their particular child, is actually present in the transference. But what we cannot know is that in attending to it we have been accurate in isolating and interpreting it. In analysis, as in life, we are left to our judgement. If I believe that the discrete communicating in a transference and my countertransference is the analysand's selective transfer of an operational logic of maternal care, then I will say so. If it proves to be the work of the ego unburdening itself of a phantasy, I think this factor will establish itself in the countertransference, as I experience the patient's more dynamically urgent need to control me for purposes of processing an unconscious phantasy. Were psychoanalysts in a position to have their internal experience printed out alongside what the patient says and does, and what the analyst says, then we might be able to sift through this evidence and differentiate the patient's transfer of phantasy or ego process as it establishes itself in the analyst's mind. That we shall never be able to do this should not deter us from leaving the reassuring comforts of the rhetorical stance of a here and now representation into the far less certain domain of the historic.

Do I conclude that the only memory of the actual world is that which is operationally learned and stored as ego structure?

Historical Sets

This brings me to a somewhat different understanding of the construction and storage of history, somewhere between the registration of the actual and the reformations of the wishful. The idea I propose is that we all possess *historical sets* which are memories of events that are bound by space and time (hence part of a set) and recurrent. They do not vary. An historical set is a cluster of memories that will always recur in relation to one another if the subject gives enough reflective time to consideration of the set.

If each of us reflects on his past, I think that we can collect our past in epochs that are bounded by space (where we were and with whom) and time (true of our lives for a distinct period). I also think that each of us has epochs that will yield sets that we are likely to have as structures in common: an early (e.g., two-to-three-year-old) set, an oedipal set, a latency set, a pre-adolescent set, and so on. But there will be considerable differences in the number of historic sets each person possesses. For example, individuals who moved frequently in childhood may have more potential sets than others, bounded by the spaces they lived in and the time they spent living there.

The creation of a set is naturally a complex, overdetermined act. I believe this is part of what I have called the conservative process, as the time lapse is part of the processing through reflection of an epoch in a child's life. Central to my understanding of this is the view that it is the child's emotional reality that is conserved, so that the eight-year-old self is holding his five-year-old self's emotional experience.

Indeed, an historic set is the construction of an earlier self, it represents the phantasies and life situations of the prior self, and it does not change. More often than not, it is precisely because it will not change that it frustrates present-day dynamic needs to shift history in the service of the self.

Am I saying that the memories we have of our past are unchangeable? No: I distinguish between those memories contained in an historical set and all other recollections. All of us can, for example, give a detailed account of our history, linking events through time. We might stop and organize such recollections within the terms of an historical set, but this is an unnoticed accomplishment. Certainly, in the course of analysis, the recovery of a memory may refer more to the here and now transference, thus distorting the past in the interest of present wishes.

An historic set is a holding space in memory, which stores the child's experience of being himself at that time in his world. I believe this conservative process is essential to living. We create sets in order to preserve the integrity of self experience, given that we have an acute sense of transformation in our being. The five year old stores his two-year-old self by creating a set because the child is changing, and losing an existential sense of the self that he once was. His construction of a set to hold prior self–other experience is a natural act, a conservative process, that stores the essence of being, to give to the construction of his psyche (his internal world) an historic depth, a matrix of material that bears the trace of the journey taken by the true self.

I have already explored how the destiny drive is the urge of the true self to find experience through which to articulate its idiom. My present interest is in the conservation of the epochal experience of the true self, the journey through space and time of the core of the person. To enable us to grasp the meaning of this concept further, I shall recollect part of an historic set of my own: the experience of the fifteen-month to three-year-old self established as a set by the time I was six or seven. This period of my life is bounded in space and time and has recurring images. My set is composed of the following image-memories:

1.   Sitting in an orange grove behind my grandparents' house,

under an orange tree, sticking my finger in the orange, squeezing the juice in my mouth, and having sticky hands.

2. Walking with my grandfather on a warm day. I have sandals on and can feel the heat coming from the sidewalk. I enjoy walking on the sidewalk because each concrete block is different and it is an adventure to step from one block to the next. Some blocks tilt down, some up. Some are cracked, and I can feel the crack under my foot. My grandfather holds my hand, which of course I have to raise, and I like his presence and his tweed suit.

3. Sitting on the ground in shorts, watching the red ants on a hot day. Liking the dirt on the ground and making figures in it.

4. Listening to the sound of the mail train at night during story time with my grandmother.

5. Hearing the bells of the local church while sitting on my grandparents' porch.

6. Playing in a closet and hiding myself inside a coat.

7. At a street corner with my mother, trying to find the family bird which has flown its coop.

8. Sitting on top of a slide at nursery school, waiting for my mother to come to collect me.

9. Having to take a compulsory nap while at school. Lying on a mattress and gazing at the wall. The unhappiness of having to be quiet.

Now the above memories constitute an historical set for me: from the age of fifteen months to three years. Every time I reflect on that time of my life, these clusters come into mind. These memories were with me by the age of nine, because I recall thinking them from that age.

These images store important states of my self at that time. They are bound by my life in Glendora, California, a sleepy rural town some forty miles south of Los Angeles. It was the terminus of the Red Street car line that went to Los Angeles, and it was surrounded by orange groves. I lived with my mother about three-quarters of a mile from her parents. My father was abroad during the war until I was twenty months old, having left when I was five months.

Each of the images conserves an important aspect of my personal being at that time. By storage of the self, I meant that each of these scenes evokes the self state depicted. I feel myself to be there again, or, the prior self now becomes an important present self experience. Each memory invokes a key object which has a concrete existence: an orange, a sidewalk, dirt, a church bell, a coat, a bird, a slide, a mattress. Small children have a more intimate relation to concrete objects than do older children and adults. They think operationally by using objects, so the objects I remember are a part of my way of thinking about my life at the time. Each of the memories also conveys the child's size *vis-à-vis* his world: I am close to the ground. Certain places are held in memory as I nominated spaces as important to me for their function: an orange grove, the sidewalk, a closet, etc.

I think the orange grove memory holds an experience of infantile sexuality, of penetrating an orally digestible object, which lies at my pleasure in a grove. Walking with my grandfather bears my experience of learning to walk, of the pleasure of doing so, and of being with a person whom I loved and who stood in for my father those first two years of my life. Playing near the ants holds another element of my infantile sexuality, as with such unfortunate creatures I no doubt exercised my sadism, or was tempted to, but I created patterns for them; perhaps their ability to fight back (they could sting!) led me to a respectful compromise. The sound of the mail train, like the sound of the church bells, holds not only my relation to the acoustic world, but signifies important objects that are far away (like fathers!) and how my grandparents' world was a soothing place for recovery from this absence.

When I recollect these memories, I can feel myself in this state again. It is this link to one's prior selves through emotional reality that to my mind is one of the distinctive functions of the historical set.

Commemoration

Although the manifest content of these memories is seemingly distress free, when I recall sitting on top of the school slide, I re-experience a lonesomeness. Equally, the compulsory nap is suffused with a blend of that sense of lonesomeness and my anger with the teachers who imposed this ritual upon me. Many memories that are part of an historical set will appear innocent of conflict, but as I

shall argue shortly, this is one of the dynamic aims of the commemoration of any moment in life: to select an experience that will
survive repression and therein store self states. Of course, some of our
historical sets will contain manifestly painful memories, and had I selected another set in my life, this would be clearer. Is it possible that
some people have no memories and no sets, because they have been
unable, as children, to create successful screen memories?

Naturally an historical set does not constitute by any means all
there is to remember of one's past. Indeed, in many respects the aim of
such conservation is not to remember details, but to conserve self
experience. In an analysis, when the patient recalls details from his
past, he may feel that he is that self during the recollected moments. If
the person is recalling a set, then he would of necessity be inside the
conserved self which was collected by the subsequent child self. This
is one of the reasons why recollecting historical sets is so important.
The adult lives again as the self remembered. He contacts the
conserved states.

The creation of an historical set is an act of considerable and complex psychic work. I am sure that such work begins before a potential
set is established. I was no doubt recalling the pleasure of the orange
groves at the time it occurred, and anticipating the sound of the mail
train was also a significant existential moment. I believe that I nominated such moments at the time as important precisely because they
contained self–other experiences that crystallized emotional reality.

A history, then, is not simply a reflective act, a retrospective. I think
we nominate here and now events as historic. We designate a
particular experience as memorable because it contains some precise
element of our personal idiom and of the world in which we live.
Certainly, this is an unconscious process, and I think the work of the
dream is important to the successful establishment of a memory
element in an historical set. To some extent, then, the dream is a crucial
'history taking' process, and this should not surprise the analyst. We
know that the dreamer creates an inner space for an unconscious
reflection on that day's lived experience – a mental processing of a unit
in space and time, a history making, that links the immediate past (the
day) with the distant past in that timeless world of unconscious
memory.

In turn, the creation of an historical set utilizes the dream to register the history of the subject's emotional reality at the time. Such an organizing of self-experience is part of a historic consciousness, as the person bears his prior self states through the conservative process of the historical set.

Thus, although the historical set may not always record the actual events of the time, it does preserve unchanged the subject's experience of life in space and time. This distinction is in my view an important one, a view that is annihilated in the sweeping notion that we can only know the here and now, and the past is only the matrix of present day wishes.

Historical Consciousness as a Mental Capacity

W hy think historically? Is it to gather biographical details alone? Valuable though reconstructions are, is this the primary function of the analyst's historicity? I think not. Historical thinking is a psychic accomplishment. It reflects an inner receptive area in the analyst that permits the analysand's development of a part of the psyche that stores self history. For me, it is important that the analyst possess a true historic consciousness, as this is a psychic function, not simply an intellectual stance. The function is as an intelligent receptor of the patient's rememberings, which will be held by the analyst. The analyst's historical orientation is less important for the history recovered than it is for the psychic reception of de-repressed memories and associations to historical sets.

We know that the stories of the past often change in the course of an analysis, but this should not deter us from continuing to create history. In fact the remaking of a history testifies to the dynamic strength of historical consciousness, as the analyst's availability as receiver of historic 'fact' allows the patient to re-present many versions of this past. A history will then be worked and reworked in an analysis, sponsoring a sense in the analysand of historic consciousness, as the work of the historian, a thinking and re-thinking of his data, is much the same endeavour as the patient's reporting of himself.

Do the analysts who regard a recollection only as a transference communication and who interpret the transference meaning rather than attend to the past neglect the development of the psychic function of historic reflection? How can the patient use an analyst to receive historical sets if this is so? Is not work of the here and now capable of simply becoming a strangely extreme form of existentialism driven by the impulse of the analyst–patient couple to refer everything that crosses the patient's mind to the analyst or the analyst and patient?

We are less familiar with the mental processes I term reception and evocation than we are with introjection and projection (Bollas, 1987). Receptive and evocative functions refer to the subject's availability for the arrival of repressed memories and for new internal objects. The receptive frame of mind is a conditional state; it depends on a relaxed, unvigilant attitude in the subject, and can be seen in analysands who are using silence to achieve an inner receptive orientation. From this position memories, daydreams, phantasies, and new internal objects are evoked. The analysand uses the analyst to hold the setting, to preserve the right of this frame of mind, and therefore is fundamentally unconcerned with the analyst as an object. Transference communicating is suspended. The ego is turned inward, to receive representations of internal psychic reality, and it is not fundamentally engaged in projective–introjective dialectics with external objects and their internal representations.

It is from the receptive process and the evocative procedure that conserved self states are lived out in the presence of the analyst. This will not occur unless the patient unconsciously perceives the analyst as prepared to allow this evolution. If the analyst fundamentally understands silence to denote resistance, then this state will not be achieved, and much that could have been discovered of the patient will be lost.

But if the analyst values the there and then, if he is willing to suspend transference interpreting momentarily, then he will enable the patient's ego to evoke mental representations of unthought knowledge.

The Resourcefulness of Screen Memory

Historical sets are forms of screen memory that accurately store a subject's experience of being during a defined historical time and within a known setting. If a child's self states are inaccurate comments on the world in which he lives, they are nonetheless profoundly accurate registrations of the child's experience of being in the world. If a patient is recollecting an historical set, it is highly likely that at the moment he is re-experiencing a prior self state. This reunion may sponsor an intense reliving of a segment in self history. In my view, it is exceedingly important that the analyst hold his tongue and simply wait until such time as the re-experiencing is completed, so that this revenant may be viewed as an object and then analysed.

I learned much from a schizophrenic patient who had never been able to recollect her past. It was too frightening and was the instigator of the hallucinogenic. However, after years of analysis she felt secure enough to remember, and what was startling to me was how she recollected simple experiences and simple objects (like a playroom, a back garden, a visit to the seashore). These rememberings were both reassuring and pleasing. Indeed, I think she was discovering the structure of historical sets, finding her self within her past. My comments were few. And over a six-month period the patient traversed her entire childhood, from the ages of three to eighteen, simply remembering and finding the historical selves contained in the historical sets. I made few interpretations during this time, although I did comment often on the pleasure, relief, and profundity she found in her recollections. Many years later I was to discover that to her this was the most valuable part of her analysis as she could rediscover the history of the self.

Certainly, however, this patient's rememberings raise interesting questions about historical sets. Why weren't her memories of traumatic moments? Why did they not depict a schizophrenic self? Why weren't they entirely suffused with pain and anguish? In fact, each memory did contain features of her distressed life and reflected ego vulnerability, but they also reflected an integrity of self experience. A self was there. Does this suggest that historical sets preserve true self states containing the subject's discrete experience of being? Are historical sets, then, resourceful internal objects? Do they testify to the true self's capacity to find pleasure, articulation, and meaning even amidst personal and family madness?

In fact, however, historical sets do bear the pain, anguish, and confusion of life. It was possible, for example, to discover the fragmented state of mind in my patient's recollections, but what distinguishes the screen memory is that part of the historical set is the storage of self within an image that is bearable. Does not this conservative process suggest a remarkable historical aim, an ego determination to preserve the self through memory, to set a limit to the unbearable, so that a history can be remembered, can be thought?

I remember, for example, the canary that flew its coop, an experience of anxiety and doubt about my mother's retrieval of the object, because in this experience I could store in manageable form my worry that my father had actually escaped the home and had flown away to his freedom. An anxiety, to be sure, which also had much to do with my oedipal wish to drive him permanently from the home and have possession of my mother and my doting grandparents without his intrusion.

A child's complete formation of an historical set follows some years after the set is completed. The three year old is not in possession of his set at the time, but by the age of five or six he will nominate several memories when asked what he remembers of his previous era. The six year old's historical set is not fully complete until the age of eight or nine. I do not know whether this is due to the neurology of memory – perhaps it is due to the transition from the hippocampal memory to long-term mnemic storage – but I do think the work of establishing the set takes time and is part of the historicizing of the present, a procedure that needs the present to become the past for commemoration to take place.

A set is not established simply to hold the history of a person's subjective life. It is also a continuing container for the subject's working through of experiences particular to the events of that time and space. We 'go into' or 're-visit' our self states contained in historical sets all the time. Recently, for example, I walked to the post office with two colleagues who are some twenty years senior to me. We walked through the quiet and picturesque village of Stockbridge: they to fetch their post, I to go for a walk. As we approached the post office, I said I would go to an adjacent store to get a copy of the *New York Times*. When I picked up my copy of the paper and moved to the cash desk, I noticed some baseball cards sold with bubble gum. Half thinking that it would be nice for my eight-year-old son, I bought them and left the store to join my colleagues. I developed a sudden taste for bubble gum and opened the package and was disappointed to find so little bubble gum inside. I was quite pleased, however, with how many baseball cards there were and hastily went through them to see if I knew any of the players. I did this while walking with my colleagues.

Now, as I look back on this event, I am sure that this emotional experience was evoked by the unconscious representation of the walk as evocative of an historic set: walking with my colleagues (like being with my grandfather), they to achieve a task (get the post), I to tag along. They the adults, I the child. As I am in a special frame of mind, I pick up baseball cards which I haven't purchased since I was a child. If I analyse this re-experiencing of a self state within an historic set, then I am sure it is occasioned by my sadness over my departure (some six months prior to writing this) from the town, the institution where I work, and my colleagues of whom I have grown very fond.

An historic set partly contains the experiences of the true self, and in turn it becomes the emotional matrix for subsequent true self articulation. A set registers the emotional experiences of the self and of those objects which facilitated true self expression and elaboration, as well as those that rebuffed this establishment of idiom. Each of these sets conserves the emotional realities of that time and partly serves as a container for the subsequent elaborative work. I cannot change my history. I can receive and evoke prior self states (particular to a period of time) and live out more fruitfully true self states therein contained.

We do not simply recollect an historical set, then, as in the past; we re-live the experience. Indeed, we are perpetually engaged in a dialectic of eras, a psychic dialectic, in which prior self states encounter present ones. In some respects, this is another way of saying something psychoanalysts already know quite well: the unconscious is timeless and contributes to the present with a status equal to the perception of reality.

Naturally every memory contained in a set is pregnant with meaning. Latent in my historical set are unconscious inscriptions of my infantile sexuality, the relation to my parents, the distribution of affects, and the selection of defences. Indeed, the psychoanalysing of such historical sets is in part a fulfilment of the aims of the conservative process: to restore self states (partly composed of unconscious phantasies) for subsequent understanding. It is as if the child knows that he needs an analyst, that at some point in a lifetime self experiences of childhood can be relived in the presence of someone who will assist the subject in understanding these states. In an analysis, such a restoration occurs along three pathways: the consideration of the patient's associations, the establishment of missing signifiers, and the patient's recreation of some of the memories within the transference.

Those memories contained in an historical set, however, do not change, even with an analysis, and in this respect they differ from other internal objects, such as the person's recollection of the mother or father, memories which indeed are subject to further de-repression, and to alteration. Perhaps this is so because the historical set is a type of screen memory and the objects of recollection are simple and not laden with intense psychic affection. The mind is not at work on them. They are simply there inside the subject like a simple memory of ordinary objects: a house, a car, etc. The simplicity of such memories, however, does not suggest a corresponding lack of profundity. Indeed they may be among the most important memories held by the person, and they are always there for remembering and for reconsideration as long as the person lives.

Visions of the Future

Does that not suggest, then, that we commemorate self states in order to ensure the preservation of our being over time? Do we have, as children, a sense of the passage of time, of its termination of our selves, as we progress through psycho-development? Do we develop then, what we might think of as historic consciousness, a sense of the function of 'taking' history so that as children we are our own historians, storing important states in our being, conserving them in sets because we know through experience that the self is changing: in its body, in its abilities, in its interests and concerns, with its objects, in the object world's multifaceted orientation to the self.

Thus as the child develops, undergoing a steady and inevitable change in his body, mental life, and social relations, he leaves behind, at each step, previous states of being, some of which seem important as containers of the essence of his life lived at that moment. My view is that knowing this, the child conserves memories, and perhaps selects relatively untroubled images that contain such experience because, unlike more disturbing experiences and their recollection, the objects of an historical set are less likely to be repressed and lost.

Indeed, I think that even as children we re-visit former states of being when we recollect an object within an historical set. It is, furthermore, an act of singular privacy and solitude. I do not think such memories are fundamentally communicable; in that the subject cannot turn them into adequate narrative representation or interpersonal realization, in much the same way that one person could not tell another about what Beethoven's Eighth Symphony sounds like. Psychoanalysis proceeds as far as it can in processing historical sets: the patient free associates, the memories link up to other sets, the patient and analyst unravel the discourse of the unconscious. But who we have been, where we have been, and with whom we have lived remain experiences which cannot be communicated to others – part of each person's essential aloneness. Perhaps this is also why we commemorate ourselves, why we conserve self states: by such conservation, we can at least maintain contact with our self, connecting our past life and past selves with what we experience currently and anticipate in the future.

One of the important functions of this type of memory, then, is its resourcefulness, its preservation of selves for intrapsychic communication. I am suggesting, further, that children store experiences for future understanding, or, to think of it differently, for future processing. I think children have a sense of their own place in psycho-developmental time; they 'know' that an experience beyond comprehension may, in time, be understood.

This orientation toward the future may simply be established through experiences of time: that over time confusions, disorientations, bewilderments, and so on are worked through, at first with the help of the parent and then with the incremental benefits of ego growth.

Do children have a vision of their future? If so, is it simply created by the parental comments on how the child is growing up, or does the child not possess an internal object which we could term the future self. Such a future self, or grown-up self, is partly constructed out of the child's sense of the greater ego adequacy of the future, in his ability to process self states that are presently beyond his ego abilities. Children, then, have an *alter ego*, not yet functioning, but there as a potential object, to arrive in the future, to which they can refer themselves. I remember as an eleven year old lying awake at night, feeling perplexed and ashamed by the fact that I was afraid to go off to war. (War may have been the eighth grade, but I didn't know this at the time.) I played football, was quite good at it, and rather heroic on the field of play, but why was I afraid of going to war? I thought I was cowardly – this was deeply shaming – but I did have a belief that when I was eighteen and the time came for me to face this fear, I would be older, maybe braver, and more able to deal with the issue. I remember telling myself to calm down and see how it turned out when I was older. Was I not referring myself to my future self? Was I not relating to an internal object, the future self, which contributed to my vision of my later years? And considering my early life, we can see that my fear of dying in a war, of wondering about my bravery, links to the war that took my father away, giving a particular character to my oedipus complex. The drive to elaborate oneself, the urge to articulate one's inner idiom or true self, which I term a destiny drive, collects material for the subject's vision of his future, and sustains an internal object, the future self, that receives many referrals to it during the course of childhood.

Our Selves in Solitude

Historical sets are internal reference libraries that make self experience available for future work. There is clearly a rich hermeneutic potential to a set, which is obvious to a practising psychoanalyst, but I hope that I have also conveyed another view: that although these memories are informative resources, conserved states of the past, and therefore of analytical use, they are also fundamentally uncommunicable and so distinct to the subject.

As Winnicott stressed again and again in his writings, we are each of us an isolate. There is an 'incommunicado element' to each person, a theme echoed in romantic literature and elsewhere. If an historical set cannot in its essence be conveyed, this is only so because we cannot share another's self experience, except, perhaps, in that moment of falling in love when it appears as if we do share direct mutual self states.

Ordinarily, however, historical sets are for us alone, and provide an important part of the culture of that internal object relation that we have to ourself as a companion. The other deeply important internal experience is obviously the dream.

In a previous chapter I suggest that essential aloneness is a positive and necessary feature of ego health, and that such aloneness may, as Winnicott speculates, emerge from the transition from non-existence to existence. If this is not a wild idea, if the foetus brings with it some trace of predependent aloneness, a personal basis for imagining our non-existence, then the solitude of our self conserving memories is a continuous 'reminder' of the ephemerality of our existence: that we do live a while, that we do bear meaning, and then we no longer exist. The intrapsychic relation to an historical set is to the 'no longer lived', to the extinct self, and selves, indeed to a small village of such deceased existents, and as we age, this internal repetition may become a valuable psycho-biological preparation for mourning the loss of life and facing the inevitability of our extinction.

By historicizing the present, by commemorating a self state for conservation, we accept the deaths of selves, inevitable in temporality itself: a past is the graveyard of all present moments. Historical sets contain the no longer present selves (and others); a sense of death is the background to the overall mood of recollecting, although the psychic aliveness of mnemic objects acts as a counterpoint, since the unconscious that knows no time is ignorant of loss and death. If the conservation of self states uses the perpetual aliveness of psychic life to sustain such a self state for us throughout our lifetime, the act of feeling and then contemplating a former self implicitly accepts the distinctness of the timekeeper's grip on our life. If this is so, then the establishment of, and relation to, historical sets is a place for the meeting up of our lives and our deaths: of life and of death. As I have said elsewhere, death to a human being is death of psyche: not the stopping of a heart or the end of brainwaves. Psychic life is only finally given a time sense by death itself. Otherwise, in looking back on former selves, we identify with the termination of our being, a valuable psycho-developmental task in coming to terms with our own final extinction.

Indeed, I think we all possess a sense of this task which partly generates the psychic economy of the destiny drive: the urge, the need to elaborate and articulate one's personal idiom through internal object relations and the use of external objects. As the subject incrementally understands the micro-lifetimes of an historical set, marked and set off to contain a distinct period of a life, the subject, as Lacan suggests, unconsciously knows his situation in terms of the *jouissance* of the true self: the right, the inalienable right, to an ecstasy that I believe is what Winnicott describes in his concept of the use of the object. That is, the subject has a sense of whether the true self is moving forward in its journey through the life span, or whether it suffers foreclosures.

The sense of selves past and the destiny drive collaborate to inspire many a person to seek a psychoanalysis (even if they have to invent a complaint to get through the analyst's door) and fortunately we are more aware than in the past of patients in late mid-life or beyond who seek analysis fundamentally because of the need to bring former selves to the other for a sustained dialogue (narrative and transferential) – a reunion of sorts, before death takes the family of selves.

Glossary

Alpha and beta elements. Terms created by Bion. Beta represents undigested mental facts that have not yet been rendered psychic. The alpha element is a specific function of the personality that transforms sense impressions into psychic elements, which are then available for mental work. For example, A walks to the store, sees fifty passers-by, and then recalls one such fellow pedestrian who reminds him of an old friend or he develops an erotic interest in the fellow traveller. The memory of erotic interest is the result of alpha function which changes this perceptual fact (one pedestrian out of fifty) into a psychical object.

Destiny drive. Refers to the urge within each person to articulate and elaborate his idiom through the selection and use of objects. It is a form of the life instinct in which the subject seeks to come into his own true being through experiencing that releases this potential.

Dialectics of difference. Refers to the generative function of disagreement between patient and analyst, in which the clinician supports the absolute right to disagree and hold different views. One function of this right, in a psychoanalysis, is to sustain the freedom of association intrinsic to the successful elaboration of unconscious knowledge.

Endopsychic perception. A term used by Freud to describe the mental representation of the structure of the mind. In cinematic terms, it is the moment when the projector casts the imagery of its internal workings on to the screen.

Eviscerative projective identification. An exceedingly quick mental act when the subject projects a part of himself into the object and then spirits off the projected content, eviscerating the recipient of any of its intrinsic characteristics. For example, A meets B in a brief moment and idealizes B. B is loved intensively by A and we may say that B contains elements of A's loving self. A continues with the projection, creating a new inner object only remotely related to B, devoid of any of B's characteristics, yet still B is housing this part of A. Or, imagine that A is watching television and sees a news programme on the effort to save the world's whale population. The television crew interviews an attractive man who is the somewhat heroic saviour of whales that have been in trouble. For a moment A loves B, but soon transforms the essence of B as an admired object into another figure, purely imaginary, who bears no resemblance to B. Let's say that B was a bearded American marine biologist who captained a research ship and that B is known for his writings on endangered species. A projects the part of A that looks after endangered parts of the self into B who is then seen as awesomely protective, but in that moment A then immediately imagines C, a bearded captain of a space ship who simply seems to be rather nice. A has eviscerated B of B's personal qualities in order to create C. This form of projective identification is typical of the ghostline personality.

Futures. The invested representation of the self and its objects in the future.

Idiom. The idiom of a person refers to the unique nucleus of each individual, a figuration of being that is like a kernel that can, under favourable circumstances, evolve and articulate. Human idiom is the defining essence of each subject, and, although all of us have some acute sense of the other's idiom, this knowledge is virtually unthinkable.

Name of the father. A concept of Lacan's that does not refer to the actual father, *per se*, but to the name of the father and to its functions, one of which is to create a signifier that separates the child from the mother. The father's name indicates an affinity with the child's progression into an independent life.

Topographic return. A mental procedure in which the subject perceives a mental object (let's say, for example, that he correctly hears a psychoanalytical interpretation), which is then 'sent' to the system unconscious where it gathers further and deeper meaning and returns to the preconscious where it is now available for a new type of consciousness enriched by this topographic journey.

Topographic reversal. Refers to a situation where the object of the subject's unconscious instinctual desire, ordinarily reflecting the rich work of unconscious displacement and symbolization, impinges on the subject driven by its own instinctual urges. For example, a child who loves the father, works on the sexual urges of this love by symbolically placing such feeling on to several objects (for example, a teddy and a family friend) which enhances the symbolic processing of instinctual life. When the father molests the child he reverses the child's symbolic representation of father love by going to the source of such love, the child's psyche–soma, there to stimulate the child with the actual object.

Transformational object. Refers to the mother's function as a processor of the infant. Known less as an actual other or as a formable internal object, the mother is nonetheless an object known through her continuous action that alters the infant's psycho-somatic being.

True self. A term used by Winnicott to refer to that inherited potential with which each person starts out in life. It is, however, not an entity (like an unconscious meaning) as it only exists in experience, upon which it is fundamentally dependent for its articulation. In some respects true self is experiencing. It refers to the nature of spontaneous action which allows for the achievement of self experiences that are the character of the true self.

Unthought known. Refers to any form of knowledge that as yet is not thought. Genetically-based knowledge – what constitutes instinctive knowledge – has not been thought out. Infants also learn rules for being and relating that are conveyed through the mother's logic of care, much of which has not been mentally processed. Children often live in family moods or practices that are beyond comprehension, even if they are partners in the living of such knowledge. Psychoanalysts, receiving patient projective identifications, come to know something, and psychoanalysis of the countertransference becomes the effort to think this knowledge.

Bibliography

The place of publication is London unless otherwise indicated.

Balint, M. (1968) *The Basic Fault*. Tavistock.

Bion, W. (1962) 'Learning from Experience', in Bion (1977), pp. 1–111.

— (1970) 'Attention and interpretation', in Bion (1977), pp. 1–131.

— (1975) *A Memoir of the Future*. Rio de Janeiro:Imago Editoria.

— (1977) *Seven Servants*. New York:Aronson.

Bollas, C. (1987) *The Shadow of the Object: Psychoanalysis of the Unthought Known*. Free Association.

Coltart, N. (1986) '"Slouching towards Bethlehem"... or thinking the unthinkable in psychoanalysis', in Kohon (1986),pp. 185–99.

Ehrenberg, D.B. (1984) 'Psychoanalytic engagement, II', *Contemp. Psychoanal.* 20:560–83.

Feiner, A.H. (1979) 'Countertransference and the anxiety of influence', in L. Epstein and A.H. Feiner, eds *Countertransference*. New York: Aronson, pp. 105–28.

Ferenczi, S. (1938) *Thalassa*. New York:Psychoanalytic Quarterly.

Freud, S. (1896) Letter to Fliess in Masson (1985), pp. 207–15.

— (1900) *The Interpretation of Dreams*, in James Strachey , ed. *The Standard Edition of the Complete Psychological Works of Sigmund Freud*, 24 vols. Hogarth, 1953-73, S.E. 4–5.

— (1913) *Totem and Taboo*. vol. 13, pp. 1–162.

— (1915) 'The unconscious'. *S.E.* 14, pp 166–214.

— (1919) 'The uncanny'. *S.E.* 17, pp. 217–53.

Giovacchini, P.L. (1972) 'The blank self' in Giovacchini (1972) *Tactics and Techniques in Psychoanalytic Therapy*. Hogarth.

— (1979) *Primitive Mental States*. New York:Aronson.

Green, A. (1983) 'The dead mother', in Green (1986), pp. 142–73.

— (1986) *On Private Madness*. Hogarth.

— (1987) *Narcissisme de vie, narcisissme de mort*. Paris: Minuit.

Heimann, P. (1956) 'Dynamics of transference representations', *Int. J. Psycho-Anal.* 37:303–10.

James, A. 'The Diary', in Murphy (1979), p. 212.

Joseph, B. (1982) 'Projective identification – some clinical aspects', in Spillius (1988), pp. 138–50.

King, P. (1978) 'Affective response of the analyst to the patient's communications', *Int. J. Psycho-Anal.* 59:329–34.

Klauber, J. (1981) *Difficulties in the Analytic Encounter*. New York:Aronson.

Klein, M. (1952) 'On observing the behaviour of young infants', in Klein (1975), pp. 94–121.

— (1975) *Envy and Gratitude and Other Works 1946–1963*. Hogarth.

Kohon, G. (1986) *The British School of Psychoanalysis: The Independent Tradition*. Free Association.

Lacan, J. (1960) 'The subversion of the subject and the dialectic of desire in the Freudian unconscious', in Lacan (1977), pp. 292–325.

— (1977) *Ecrits*. Tavistock.

Laplanche, J. and Pontalis, J.-B. (1973) *The Language of Psycho-Analysis*. Hogarth.

Limentani, A. (1981) 'The negative therapeutic reaction', *Int. J. Psycho-Anal.* 62:379–90.

— (1986) 'Variations on some Freudian themes', *Int. J. Psycho-Anal.* 67:235–43.

Little, M. (1981) *Transference Neurosis and Transference Psychosis*. New York:Aronson; Free Association/Maresfield Library, 1986.

McDougall, J. (1980) *Plea for a Measure of Abnormality*. New York: International Universities Press.

— (1985) *Theatres of the Mind*. New York:Basic Books; Free Association, 1986.

Masson, J. M., ed. (1985) *The Complete Letters of Sigmund Freud to Wilhelm Fliess 1887–1904*. Harvard University Press.

Milner, M. (1988) *The Hands of the Living God*. Virago.

Murphy, E. (1979) *The Macmillan Treasury of Relevant Quotations*. Macmillan.

Pedder, J.R. (1976) 'Attachment and new beginning', *Int. Rev. Psycho-Anal*. 3:491–7.

Pontalis, J.-B. (1981) 'Between the dream as object and the dream-text', in *Frontiers in Psychoanalysis*. Hogarth, pp. 23–55.

Racker, H. (1957) 'The meanings and uses of countertransfrence', in *Transference and Countertransference* (1968), Hogarth, pp. 127–73.

Reik, T. (1956) *The Search Within*. New York: Minerva.

Rosenfeld, H. (1987) *Impasse and Interpretation*. Tavistock.

Searles, H. (1965) *Collected Papers on Schizophrenia and Related Subjects*. New York:International Universities Press.

Seldes, G. (1985) *The Great Thoughts*. New York:Ballantine.

Spillius, E.B. (1988) *Melanie Klein Today*. Tavistock.

Staël, Madame de, in Seldes (1985), p. 397.

Stewart, H. (1985) 'Changes of inner space', *Int. J. Psycho-Anal*. 68:255–64.

Symington, N. (1983) 'The analyst's act of freedom as agent of therapeutic change', in Kohon (1986), pp. 253–70

Tustin, F. (1981) *Autistic States in Children*. Routledge & Kegan Paul.

Winnicott, D.W. (1941) 'The observation of infants in a set situation', in Winnicott (1975), pp. 52–69.

— (1947) 'Hate in the countertransference', in Winnicott (1975), pp. 194–203.

— (1954) 'Metapsychological and clinical aspects of regression within the psycho-analytical set-up', in Winnicott (1975), pp. 278–94.

— (1960) 'The theory of the parent–infant relationship', in Winnicott (1972), pp. 37–55.

— (1963) 'Communicating and not communicating leading to a study of certain opposites', in Winnicott (1972), pp. 179–92.

— (1968) 'Sum, I am', in Winnicott (1986), pp. 55–64.

— (1969) 'The use of an object and relating through identifications', in Winnicott (1971), pp. 86–94.

— (1971) *Playing and Reality*. Tavistock.

— (1972) *The Maturational Process and the Facilitating Environment*. Hogarth.

— (1975) *Through Pediatrics to Psychoanalysis*. Hogarth.

— (1986) *Home is Where We Start From.* Harmondsworth:Penguin.
— (1988) *Human Nature.* Free Association.

Index

This first edition of
Forces of Destiny: Psychoanalysis and Human Idiom
was finished in June 1989.

It was set in 10/13 Palatino Roman
on a Linotron 202
printed on a Miller TP41
on to 80 g/m^2 vol. 18
New Edition Cream Antique wove.

The book was commissioned and edited by Robert M. Young,
copy-edited by Alison Wertheimer,
indexed by Susan Ramsey,
designed by Wendy Millichap
and produced by Martin Klopstock and Selina O'Grady
for Free Association Books.